ADDICTED TO WAR

Why the U.S. Can't Kick Militarism

an illustrated exposé
by Joel Andreas

Requests to reprint all or part of *Addicted to War* should be addressed to:

Frank Dorrel	AK Press (US)	AK Press (UK)
P.O. Box 3261	674-A 23rd Street	PO Box 12766
Culver City, CA 90231-3261	Oakland, CA 94612-1163	Edinburgh, EH8 9YE
(310) 838-8131	USA	Scotland, UK
fdorrel@addictedtowar.com	akpress@akpress.org	ak@akedin.demon.co.uk
www.addictedtowar.com	www.akpress.org	www.akuk.com

To order more copies:

For information about ordering more copies of *Addicted to War,* contact either Frank Dorrel or AK Press. ***Please ask about bulk rates!*** *Addicted to War* is also available through your local bookstore and online book dealers. To receive an AK Press catalog, please write or visit the AK Press website.

To order *Addicted to War* in other languages:

Addicted to War is now available in Japanese and will soon be available in Korean, Spanish, and other languages. If you live in the United States, you can order copies of *Addicted to War* in other languages from Frank Dorrel. If you live in Japan, you can buy the Japanese edition from your local bookstore or you can order it from the Global Peace Campaign (www.peace2001.org).

Teaching guide available:

To get a guide for teachers, including sample questions for each chapter, send $2 to Frank Dorrel.

Table of Contents

Sources are listed starting on page 66 and are referenced throughout the book with circled numbers. All quotes in "quotation marks" are actual quotes.

Author's Preface to the 2003 Edition

I wrote and illustrated the first edition of *Addicted to War* following the first U.S. war against Iraq in 1992. The people of this country had been largely shielded from the truth about that and previous wars waged by the United States. My aim was to present information difficult to find in the mainstream news media (which had been largely reduced to wartime cheerleaders). I also wanted to explain this country's extraordinary predilection to go to war. As this edition goes to press, this chronic U.S. addiction to war has reached a new level of intensity. The Bush/Cheney administration is now gearing up for a new war against Iraq. A thin rhetorical veneer about combating terrorism and the proliferation of weapons of mass destruction hardly conceals the main aims of the war: to impose a U.S. client regime in the heart of the Middle East and assure control over a country that has the second largest known oil reserves in the world. It is also clear that Washington intends to inflict terrible death and destruction on the Iraqi people as an example to back up aggressive threats against other countries.

The domestic costs of this addiction are being felt more acutely. As military spending skyrockets, huge government budget deficits have reappeared, threatening a new round of sharp cuts in domestic programs, including education, medical care, housing, public transportation, and environmental protection. The "war on terrorism" is also being used as an excuse to step up police surveillance of people in the U.S.

In this edition I have only updated military spending statistics and made a few small corrections. Many readers suggested that the book close with ideas about what we can do to end America's addiction to war. In response, we have added a list of organizations conducting anti-war education and activities.

Many people helped create and distribute this book. It is impossible to thank them all here. Instead, I will mention only three: My mother, Carol Andreas, who introduced me to anti-war activities; my father, Carl Andreas, who originally encouraged me to write the book; and Frank Dorrel, whose tireless promotion made a new edition both possible and irresistible.

Joel Andreas, February 2003

Publisher's Note

I first read the original 1992 edition of *Addicted to War* two years ago. My immediate response was to buy 100 copies. That's how good I thought it was. Then I learned it was out of print. I located the author, Joel Andreas, and convinced him to update the book. In April 2002, I published a new edition with the help of AK Press. The response has been tremendous. In nine months, over 45,000 copies have been distributed.

Addicted to War is being used as a textbook by many high school and college teachers. Peace organizations are selling the book at anti-war rallies, teach-ins, and smaller events. It is showing up in schools, churches, and public libraries. More and more bookstores are carrying it, including progressive independents, national chains, and comic book stores. Individuals are ordering multiple copies to give to friends, co-workers, and relatives. I have received thousands of calls, email messages, and letters from people telling me how much they love this book! *Addicted to War* has become a best seller in Japan and it will soon be available in Spanish and Korean. Editions in other languages are in the works. We are producing a CD-ROM version and a production studio has started making an animated documentary video. Others are working on a radio play and a stage production has been proposed. All these versions are helping get the book's anti-war message out to greater numbers of people around the world.

I want to thank Joel Andreas for giving us a powerful educational tool that reveals the sad and painful truth about U.S. militarism. Thanks to Yumi Kikuchi for her support and for making the Japanese edition of *Addicted to War* possible. We are honored that some of America's most courageous peace educators and activists have endorsed the book. Special thanks to my friends, to my family, and to S. Brian Willson, for supporting this project from the beginning. Finally, I want to thank you, the reader, for your concern about the issues addressed in this book. I encourage you to use it to help bring about a change of consciousness in this country. Please consider taking a copy to a teacher who might use it in class. Take a copy to your church, synagogue, or mosque. Send one to your congressperson, city council member, or someone in the media. Show it to friends and family. Education is the key. It's up to each of us to do our part. People around the world are counting on us to end our country's addiction to war.

Frank Dorrel, February 2003

The United States maintains the largest and **most powerful military in history.** U.S. warships dominate the oceans, its missiles and bombers can strike targets on every continent, and hundreds of thousands of U.S. troops are stationed overseas. Every few years the U.S. sends soldiers, warships and warplanes to **fight in distant countries.** Many countries go to war, but the U.S. is **unique** in both the **size and power** of its military and its **propensity to use it.**

The **costs** of being a **military superpower** and **waging wars** around the world are high. Because hundreds of billions of dollars are funneled to the Pentagon every year, the government skimps on providing for **basic needs** of people here at home. **Cutbacks in social programs** have caused far **more devastation** in this country than any **foreign army** ever has.

MILLION $ A MINUTE

CITY OF GREENSBU

JEFFERSON COUNTY HOSPITAL

WASHINGTON ELEMENTARY SCHOOL

Foreign wars also bring **bloody retaliation** against the U.S. — such as the **terrorist attacks** that took the lives of thousands of people at the **Pentagon** and the **World Trade Center.**

Despite the high costs in **money and lives,** the government seems determined to keep going to war, **putting us all in harm's way!**

But the costs of U.S. foreign wars are more than simply economic. They include the **lives of the soldiers** who never come home.

But **why** is the United States always **getting into wars?**

To answer that, you have to understand the **history** of this country

Two centuries ago, the United States was a collection of **thirteen small colonies** on the Atlantic coast of North America. Today it **dominates the globe** in a way that even the most powerful of past empires could not have imagined.

The path to world power has **not** been **peaceful**

I'll have to read up on this...

Chapter 1
"Manifest Destiny"

The **American revolutionaries** who rose up against **King George** in 1776 spoke eloquently about the **right of every nation to determine its own destiny.**

"When in the course of human events it becomes necessary for one people to **dissolve** the political bands which have connected them with another, and assume, among the **Powers of the earth**, the separate and equal station to which the Laws of Nature and of Nature's God **entitle them...**"

Thomas Jefferson, from the Declaration of Independence, 1776

Unfortunately, after they won the right to determine **their own destiny** they thought they should determine **everyone else's too!**

The leaders of the **newly independent colonies** believed that they were **preordained** to rule all of North America. This was so obvious to them that they called it **"Manifest Destiny."**

② ③

"We must march from **ocean to ocean**. ...It is the destiny of the **white race.**"

Representative Giles of Maryland

This "manifest destiny" soon led to genocidal wars against the **Native American peoples**. The U.S. Army ruthlessly **seized** their land, driving them west and slaughtering those who resisted.

During the century that followed the American Revolution, the Native American peoples were defeated one by one, their lands were taken, and they were confined to **reservations**. The number of dead has never been counted. But the tragedy did not end with the dead. The Native peoples' **way of life** was devastated. ③ ④

"I can still see the butchered women and children lying heaped and scattered all along the crooked gulch as plain as when I saw them with eyes still young. And I can see that something else died there in the bloody mud, and was buried in the blizzard. A **people's dream** died there. It was a beautiful dream ...the nation's hoop is **broken and scattered.**"

Black Elk, spiritual leader of the Lakota people and survivor of the Wounded Knee massacre in South Dakota

By 1848 the United States had seized **nearly half of Mexico's territory.**

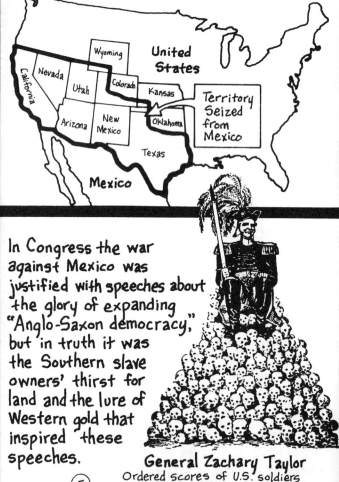

California
Nevada
Utah
Wyoming
Colorado
Kansas
United States
Arizona
New Mexico
Oklahoma
Texas
Territory Seized from Mexico
Mexico

In Congress the war against Mexico was justified with speeches about the glory of expanding "Anglo-Saxon democracy," but in truth it was the Southern slave owners' thirst for land and the lure of Western gold that inspired these speeches.

General Zachary Taylor
Ordered scores of U.S. soldiers executed for refusing to fight in Mexico.

⑤

④

With their domain now stretching from **coast to coast** the "Manifest Destiny" crowd began to dream of an **overseas empire**. Economic factors drove these ambitions. Col. Charles Denby, a railroad magnate and an ardent **expansionist**, argued:

"Our condition at home is **forcing** us to commercial expansion... Day by day, **production is exceeding home consumption**... We are after markets, the greatest **markets** in the world."

⑥

Calls for **empire** were echoing through the halls of Washington.

"I firmly believe that when any territory outside the **present territorial limits** of the United States becomes necessary for our defense or essential for our commercial development, we ought to **lose no time** in acquiring it."

Senator Orville Platt
of Connecticut, 1894

⑦

To become a world power the U.S. built a **world-class navy**. A gung-ho Theodore Roosevelt was put in charge of it.

⑧

"I should **welcome** almost **any war**, for I think this country **needs one**."

T. Roosevelt, 1897

He didn't have **long** to wait.

The next year, taking a fancy to several Spanish colonies, including **Cuba and the Philippines**, the U.S. declared war on Spain. **Rebel armies** were already fighting for **independence** in both countries and Spain was on the verge of defeat. Washington declared that it was on the rebels' side and Spain quickly capitulated. But the U.S. soon made it clear that it had **no intention of leaving**.

⑨

"The Philippines are **ours forever**... and just beyond the Philippines are China's illimitable markets ... the Pacific is **our ocean**."

Senator Albert Beveridge
of Indiana, 1900

And for the Senator, the Pacific was **only the beginning**:

"The power that rules the Pacific is the power that **rules the world**... That power is and will forever be the American Republic."

⑩

Elaborate **racist theories** were invented to **justify colonialism** and these theories were adopted enthusiastically in Washington.

"We are the **ruling race of the world**. ...We will not renounce our part in the mission of our race, **trustee, under God** of the civilization of the world. ...He has marked us as **his chosen people**... He has made us **adept in government** that we may administer government among **savage and senile peoples**." ⑪

Senator Albert Beveridge, again

But the Filipinos didn't share the views of Senator Beveridge and his buddies.

They fought the new invaders just as they had fought the Spanish. The U.S. subjugated the Philippines with brute force. U.S. soldiers were ordered to "**Burn all and kill all**," and they did. By the time the Filipinos were defeated, **600,000 had died.** ⑫

U.S. soldiers stand on the bones of Filipinos who died in the war

The **Philippines, Puerto Rico,** and **Guam** were made into **U.S. colonies** in 1898. Cuba was formally given its independence, but along with it the Cubans were given the Platt Ammendment, which stipulated that the **U.S. Navy** would operate a base in Cuba **forever,** that the U.S. Marines would **intervene at will,** and that Washington would determine Cuba's foreign and financial policies.

Now, don't say I never gave you anything.

Independence

Platt Amendment ⑬

During the same period, the U.S. **overthrew Hawaii's Queen Liliuokalani** and transformed these unspoiled Pacific islands into a **U.S. Navy base** surrounded by Dole and Del Monte plantations. In 1903, after Theodore Roosevelt became president, he sent **gunboats** to secure **Panama's** separation from Colombia. The Colombian government had refused Roosevelt's terms for building **a canal.** (14)

If they won't sell, I'll just take it!

Then Uncle Sam began sending his Marines **everywhere**

The Marines went to China, Russia, North Africa, Mexico, Central America, and the Caribbean. (15)

♫ From the Halls of Montezuma to the shores of Tripoli... ♫

Troops march in Siberia during the U.S. invasion of Russia, 1918

Between 1898 and 1934, the Marines invaded Cuba 4 times, Nicaragua 5 times, Honduras 7 times, the Dominican Republic 4 times, Haiti twice, Guatemala once, Panama twice, Mexico 3 times, and Colombia 4 times! (16)

In many countries, the Marines stayed on as an **occupying army**, sometimes for decades. When the Marines finally went home, they typically left the countries they had occupied in the hands of a **friendly dictator**, armed to the teeth to suppress his own people.

Behind the Marines came **legions of U.S. business executives** ready not only to sell their goods but also to set up **plantations**, drill **oil wells**, and stake out **mining claims**. The Marines returned when called upon to enforce **slave-like working conditions** and put down **strikes, protests, and rebellions.**

(17)

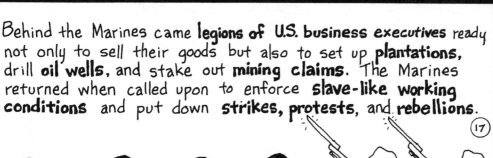

Standard Oil | United Fruit | Domino Sugar | Anaconda Copper

"[I accept responsibility for] active intervention to secure for **our capitalists** opportunity for **profitable investments.**"

(18)

President William Howard Taft, 1910

A reporter described what took place after U.S. troops landed in **Haiti in 1915** to put down a **peasant rebellion**:

American marines opened fire with machine guns from airplanes on defenseless Haitian villages, killing men, women and children in the open market places for sport.

(19) (20)

50,000 Haitians were killed.

General Smedley Butler was one of the most celebrated leaders of these **Marine expeditions.** After he retired, he reconsidered his career, describing it as follows:

"I spent 33 years and 4 months in active **military service...** And during that period I spent most of my time as a **high-class muscle man for Big Business,** for Wall Street and the bankers. In short, I was a racketeer, a **gangster for capitalism.**"

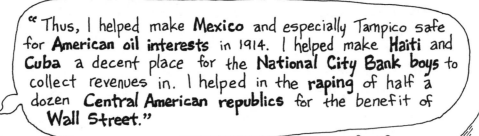

"Thus, I helped make **Mexico** and especially Tampico safe for **American oil interests** in 1914. I helped make **Haiti** and **Cuba** a decent place for the **National City Bank boys** to collect revenues in. I helped in the **raping** of half a dozen **Central American republics** for the benefit of **Wall Street.**"

"I helped **purify Nicaragua** for the international banking house of **Brown Brothers** in 1902-1912. I brought light to the **Dominican Republic** for American sugar interests in 1916. I helped make **Honduras** right for **American fruit companies** in 1903. In **China** in 1927, I helped see to it that **Standard Oil** went on its way unmolested."

(21)

U.S. Marine officer with the head of Silvino Herrera, one of the leaders of Augusto Sandino's rebel army, Nicaragua, 1930

World War I was a horrific battle among the European colonial powers over how to divide up the world.

When President Woodrow Wilson decided to **enter the fray**, he told the American people that he was sending troops to Europe to "**make the world safe for democracy.**"

The Chicago Daily Tribune. FINAL EDITION

U.S. AT WAR: WILSON

U-BOAT SINKS AZTEC. ARMED U.S. STEAMER

NOW FOR THE DEEDS

WARNINGS TO GERMANY!

BOTH HOUSES HASTEN WORK ON PROGRAM

"WE MUST FIGHT FOR JUSTICE AND RIGHTS"

But what Wilson was **really after** was what he considered to be the United States' **fair share of the spoils.**

Wilson's ambassador to England said rather forthrightly that the U.S. would declare war on Germany because it was...

(22)

"... the **only way** of maintaining our present **pre-eminent trade status.**"

Ambassador W.H. Page, 1917

For this, **130,274** U.S. soldiers were **sent to their deaths.** (23)

"Our boys were sent off to die with **beautiful ideals** painted in front of them. No one told them that **dollars and cents** were the real reason they were marching off to **kill and die.**" (24)

General Smedley Butler, 1934

World War I was supposed to be the "war to end all wars."

It wasn't.

During **World War II**, millions of young Americans signed up to fight **German fascism** and **Japanese imperialism.** But the goals of the strategic planners in Washington were far **less admirable.**

They had **imperial ambitions** of their own.

In October 1940, as German and Japanese troops were **marching in Europe and Asia**, a group of **prominent government officials, business executives, and bankers** was convened by the U.S. State Department and the Council on Foreign Relations to discuss U.S. strategy. They were concerned with maintaining an **Anglo-American "sphere of influence"** that included the British Empire, the Far East, and the Western hemisphere. They concluded that the country had to **prepare for war** and come up with...

"...an integrated policy to achieve **military and economic supremacy** for the United States."

Yes! Yes! Yes!

(25)

Of course, they didn't say this **publicly**.

If war aims are stated which seem to be concerned solely with Anglo-American imperialism, they will offer little to people in the rest of the world... The interests of other peoples should be stressed... This would have a better propaganda effect. (26)

From a private memorandum between the Council on Foreign Relations and the State Department, 1941

A horrendous war was concluded with a horrendous event: **200,000 people were killed** instantaneously when the U.S. dropped **nuclear bombs** first on **Hiroshima** and then on **Nagasaki**. Tens of thousands more died later from radiation poisoning.

(27)

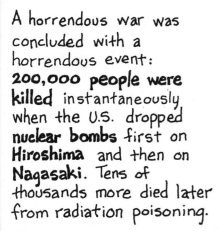

"We pray that God might guide us to use [the Bomb] in **His** ways and for **His purposes**."

President Harry Truman, 1945

(28)

The defeat of Japan had already been assured **before** the bombs were dropped. Their main purpose was to **demonstrate** to the world the deadly power of America's new **weapon of mass destruction**.

(29)

World War II left the U.S. in a position of **political, economic** and **military superiority**.

" We must set the pace and assume the responsibility of the **majority stockholder** in this **corporation known as the world**."

Leo Welch, former Chairman of the Board, Standard Oil of New Jersey (now Exxon) 1946

(30)

The U.S. eagerly **assumed responsibility** for determining the economic policies and selecting the management of what it considered to be the **subsidiary companies** that made up the "**corporation known as the world**."

But this didn't go over too well in many nations that considered themselves to be **sovereign countries**.

FUERA YANKIS!

Boy, I never read about **any** of that stuff in **here**!

AMERICA Land of Freedom

Chapter 2

The "Cold War" and the Exploits of the Self-Proclaimed "World Policeman"

Go ahead— make my day!

World Cop

The United States, however, had to contend with the **Soviet Union**, which had also emerged from the Second World War as a **world power.** For the next 45 years, the world was caught up in a global turf battle between the "**two superpowers.**" The U.S. was always much stronger than its Soviet adversary, but both countries maintained huge military forces to defend and expand their own "**spheres of influence.**" The contention between the two powers was called the "**Cold War**" because they never directly engaged each other in battle. But the "Cold War" was marked by plenty of violence in other countries. Typically, the two superpowers lined up on **opposite sides** of every conflict.

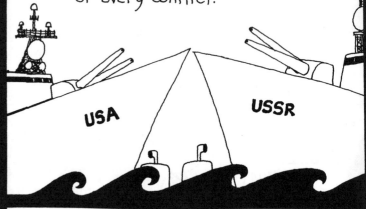

USA   USSR

For its part, the U.S. moved to expand its own "sphere of influence" beyond the Americas and the Pacific to include much of the **old British, French** and **Japanese colonial empires** in **Asia** and **Africa.** In doing so, it had to deal with local aspirations that did not always accord with American plans. To put down insubordination, disorder and disloyalty in its sphere, the new "**majority stockholder**" also appointed itself the "**world policeman.**" During the Cold War, Washington **intervened** militarily in foreign countries more than **200 times.**

③

Don't mess with the U.S.A., buster!

Korea, 1950-1953

After World War II, the **ambitious plans** of the U.S. State Department for Asia and the Pacific were upset completely by **revolutions and anti-colonial wars** from China to Malaysia. A major confrontation developed in **Korea**. Washington decided to intervene directly to show that **Western military technology** could defeat **any Asian army.**

We'll show these #@¿%$!

U.S. warships, bombers, and artillery reduced much of Korea to **rubble.** Over **4,500,000 Koreans died**; three out of four were **civilians. 54,000 U.S. soldiers returned home in coffins.** But the U.S. military, for all of its technological superiority, **did not prevail.** After 3 years of intense warfare, a cease-fire was negotiated. Korea is still divided and some 40,000 U.S. troops remain in southern Korea to this day.

Waiting for another war.

(32)

Dominican Republic, 1965

After a **U.S.-backed military coup,** Dominicans rose up to demand the reinstatement of the overthrown president (who they had elected in a popular vote). Washington, however, was determined to keep its men in power, **no matter who the Dominicans voted for.** 22,000 U.S. troops were sent to suppress the uprising. 3,000 people were **gunned down** in the streets of Santo Domingo.

(33)

YANKEES GO HOME

Vietnam, 1964-1973

For ten years the U.S. assaulted Vietnam with all the deadly force the Pentagon could muster, trying to preserve a **corrupt South Vietnamese regime**, which had been inherited from the **French colonial empire**. The U.S. may have used **more firepower** in Indochina (Vietnam, Laos, and Cambodia) than had been used by **all sides** in **all previous wars** in human history.

> Sometimes you have to **destroy a** country to **save** it.

U.S. warplanes dropped **seven million tons** of bombs on Vietnam.

> That's the equivalent of one 350-pound bomb **per person!**

Despite the ferocity of the assault on Vietnam, the U.S. was ultimately defeated by a **lightly armed but determined** peasant army. (34)

400,000 tons of napalm were rained down on the tiny country. **Agent Orange** and other toxic herbicides were used to destroy millions of acres of farmland and forests. Villages were burned to the ground and their residents massacred. Altogether, **two million people died** in the Indochina War, most of them civilians killed by U.S. bombs and bullets. Almost **60,000 U.S. soldiers were killed** and 300,000 wounded.

14

Lebanon, 1982-1983

After the Israeli invasion of Lebanon, the U.S. Marines intervened directly in the **Lebanese civil war**, taking the side of Israel and the right-wing Falange militia.

Which had just massacred 2000 Palestinian civilians.

U.S. Marines marching into Beirut, 1983

241 Marines paid for this intervention with their lives when their barracks were blown up by a **truck bomb**.
(35)

Grenada, 1983

About **110,000 people** live on the tiny Caribbean island of **Grenada**.

About the same number that live in **Peoria, Illinois.**

But, according to **Ronald Reagan**, Grenada represented a **threat to U.S. security**. So he ordered the Pentagon to seize the island and install a new government **more to his liking**.
(36)

" A **lovely** piece of **real estate**."

Secretary of State George Schultz, 1983
(37)

I'm a Bechtel man and a Pentagon fan

Libya, 1986

Washington loved **King Idris**, the Libyan monarch who happily turned over his country's **oil reserves** to Standard Oil for **next to nothing**. It hates **Col. Qadhafi**, who threw the King out. In 1986, Reagan ordered U.S. warplanes to bomb the Libyan capital, Tripoli, claiming that Qadhafi was responsible for a bomb attack at a German disco that **killed two U.S. soldiers**. It's unlikely that very many of the hundreds of Libyans killed or injured in the U.S. bombing raid **knew anything** about the German bombing.

The nerve of those terrorists — **bombing those poor people!**

(38)

So far we've recounted wars that have **involved U.S. troops**.

But there are many **other wars** in which Washington is involved **behind the scenes**.

After World War II, Britain was compelled to dispose of its **colonial empire** in the Middle East. It decided to give a big chunk of the land known as **Palestine** to **European Jews** displaced by the **Holocaust**. The problem was that there were already people living there. The result has been five decades of violence and war. Hundreds of thousands of Palestinians were **driven from their homes** in what became Israel. The center of the conflict has been the **West Bank** and **Gaza**, where Palestinians have lived for decades under **Israeli occupation**.

The U.S. provides crucial political support and billions of dollars a year in aid to Israel, including the most **advanced weaponry**. More than three decades of occupation of the West Bank and Gaza have produced bitter anger not only at Israel but also at the United States. As **Palestinian teenagers** continue to die in confrontations with the **Israeli Army** this anger only grows.

Made in USA

(39)

The U.S. government stands behind its friends – including dictatorial regimes suppressing their own people. In the 1970s and '80s **popular insurgencies** challenged corrupt dictatorships in **Central America**. The Pentagon and the CIA armed and trained security forces and death squads that killed hundreds of thousands of people, mostly **unarmed peasants**, in Nicaragua, El Salvador, and Guatemala.

(40)

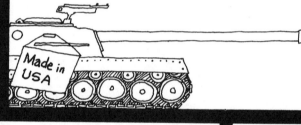

Don't believe them – they were terrorists **disguised as peasants!**

Many of the military officers responsible for the **worst atrocities** in Central America were trained at the Pentagon's **"School of the Americas"** in Georgia. The School trains officers from all over Latin America. Its training manuals recommend **torture** and **summary execution**. Its graduates have returned to establish military regimes and **terrorize** their own people.

CLOSE the School of Assassins

NO MORE TORTURE TRAINING

(41)

Fort Benning is a Terrorist Training Camp

Today bloody U.S.-backed counter-insurgency wars continue in **Colombia, Mexico, Peru**, the **Philippines** and other countries. In Colombia, a corrupt U.S.-backed army fights alongside paramilitary forces that have **slaughtered whole villages** and hundreds of opposition **union leaders** and **politicians**. The U.S. has been getting more deeply involved, under the cover of the **"War on Drugs,"** providing billions of dollars of arms used to continue the killing.

(42)

US   US

The CIA and the Pentagon have also organized **proxy armies** to overthrow governments that are **not well-liked in Washington**. In 1961, for instance, U.S. warships ferried **a small army of mercenaries** to Cuba, hoping to reverse the **Cuban Revolution**. They landed at the **Bay of Pigs**.

We'll **show 'em!**

Cubano

It was the **fifth U.S. invasion** of Cuba this century. But this time the U.S. was **defeated**.

(43)

BOOM

In the 1970s and '80s, the **CIA** was **particularly busy** financing, training and arming **guerrilla armies** around the world

For years the U.S. backed Portugal's efforts to hang on to its **colonies in southern Africa**, helping it stave off independence wars in **Angola** and **Mozambique**.

In 1975, after a democratic revolution in Portugal, the Portuguese **called it quits**.

But Washington didn't!

Instead, it teamed up with the **apartheid regime** in South Africa to supply a **mercenary army** to fight the new government in independent Angola. And in Mozambique, top U.S. and South African politicians and ex-military officers sponsored a **particularly brutal bunch** of mercenaries who massacred tens of thousands of peasants. (44)

Democracy!

Freedom!

USA

South African Apartheid Regime

(17)

And then, of course, there are the "contras."

After the **Nicaraguan people** overthrew the U.S.-backed dictatorship of the Somoza family in 1979, the CIA gathered together the **remnants of Somoza's hated National Guard** and sent them back to Nicaragua with all the weapons they could carry— to **loot, burn, and kill.**

"[The contras are] the **moral equivalent** of our founding fathers."

Ronald Reagan, 1985

45

I'm a contra too!

In 1979, the Soviet Union invaded **Afghanistan** to prop up a friendly regime. **Soviet occupation** met **fierce popular resistance.** The CIA stepped in to arm, finance and train the Afghan **mujahedin guerrillas,** working closely with the Pakistani and Saudi governments. With generous support from Washington and its allies, the mujahedin defeated the Soviets after a **brutal decade-long war.**

46

Among the CIA's collaborators in this war was a Saudi named **Osama bin Laden.** Together with the CIA, bin Laden supplied the Afghan mujahedin with money, and guns to fight the Soviets. The Afghan war helped **militarize** an **international Islamic movement** to rid the Muslim world of foreign domination. Ultimately, this movement didn't like the **United States** any more than the **Soviets.** At that time, however, the U.S. backers of bin Laden and the mujahedin were not overly concerned about their wider goals.

47

We will drive **all infidel troops** from Muslim lands!

That's right! Let's whip the **Evil Empire!**

USA

In the 1980s, Reagan **stepped up the arms race**, increasing military spending to unprecedented levels. The Soviets, with a much smaller economy, **struggled to keep up.**

Two can play **this** game!

USSR

But they couldn't. Massive military spending put **tremendous strain** on Soviet society, contributing to its **collapse.** The U.S. **won the arms race** and the **Cold War.**

As the Cold War came to an end, some people began talking about an "**era of world peace**" and a "**peace dividend.**" But behind closed doors at the White House and the Pentagon the talk was quite different.

They were busy planning a **new era of wars**

NEW WORLD ORDER

We won!

Chapter 3
The
"New World Order"

In 1989, as the "Eastern Bloc" began to **crumble**, George H. Bush gathered together his **national security advisors** to discuss the world situation. The Soviet Union, they happily agreed, was no longer **able or inclined** to counter U.S. military intervention abroad. It was time, they decided, to **demonstrate U.S. military power** to the world. The White House wanted some **decisive victories.**

Much Weaker Enemy.

Much Weaker Enemy

Yes!

Yes!

Yes!

"In cases where the U.S. confronts **much weaker enemies,** our challenge will be not simply to defeat them, but to defeat them **decisively and rapidly.**"

From a National Security Council policy review document, 1989

48

Panama, 1989

Panama was the first country selected to be the "**much weaker enemy**."

Ever since **U.S. warships** brought Panama into existence, U.S. troops have intervened in the small country whenever Washington deemed it necessary. George **Bush** continued this **tradition** in 1989, sending in **25,000 troops.**

Supposedly to arrest a drug dealer.

The drug charges were only a pretext. The real motive was assuring U.S. control over the **Panama Canal** and the extensive **U.S. military bases** in that country. A **new Panamanian president** was sworn in at a U.S. air base moments before the invasion. Hardly "Mr. Clean," the man the U.S. State Department picked for the job, Guillermo Endara, ran a bank that is notorious for **money laundering.**

(49)

We believe in **free enterprise!**

Of course, not only Panamanian banks are involved in this business. Most **big U.S. banks** have set up branches in Panama City.

(50)

Gotta get a piece of the action!

And drug trafficking and money laundering have **increased** sharply in Panama since "**Operation Just Cause.**"

(51)

Aduana/Customs

Cocaine

According to Panamanian human rights groups, **several thousand people were killed** in the U.S. invasion. 26 were U.S. soldiers. 50 were Panamanian soldiers. The rest were **civilians**, cut down by the overwhelming U.S. firepower poured into **crowded neighborhoods** in poor sections of Panama City and Colón.

Many of the dead were put in **garbage bags** and **secretly buried** in mass graves.

(52)

Iraq, 1991

Only 13 months after the U.S. invaded Panama, it went to war again — this time on a much larger scale. Like always, the government's PR department was called upon to convince us that the war against Iraq was about **freedom and justice**. But **almost everyone** knows what it was **really** about.

"Even a **dolt** understands the principle — we **need the oil**."

(53)

Advisor to G.H.W. Bush, **Time** magazine, 1990

Long ago, the U.S. State Department declared that **Middle East oil** was:

" a stupendous source of **strategic power**... one of the **greatest prizes** in world history."

(54)

65% of the world's known oil reserves lie in the Middle East. Control over the flow of this oil by U.S. oil companies has given the U.S. strategic power over Europe, Japan and the developing world. Washington thinks of the Middle East oil fields as its own **private reserves**, proclaiming them to be among its " **vital interests**."

(55)

"**Oil** is much **too important** a commodity to be **left in the hands** of the **Arabs**"

(56)

Henry Kissinger

What are you up to?

Exploring to see if there are any **vital American interests** under your soil.

Mobil

(21)

The U.S. government had been planning for the Persian Gulf War **since 1979,** when President Carter set up the **"Rapid Deployment Force"** and declared that **any threat** to Persian Gulf oil...

*"... will be repelled by **any means necessary,** including military force."*

Jimmy Carter, 1979

In the early 1980's **Iran** was seen as the main threat to **U.S. "interests"** in the Gulf, so Washington and its allies **supported** the **Iraqi invasion** of **Iran** and provided the Iraqi military with **lots of high-tech weapons** to pound their neighbor. U.S. companies even sold Iraq materials to make **chemical and biological weapons,** including **anthrax.** The Pentagon supplied satellite photos of Iranian troop deployments and then looked the other way when Iraq bombarded them with **poison gas.**

Don't do anything I wouldn't do!

Anthrax

TOXIC CHEMICALS

TOXIC CHEMICALS

In 1987, the Reagan administration intervened directly in the Iran-Iraq War (on Iraq's side), sending a **naval armada** to the Persian Gulf to protect the oil tankers of a country that was then Iraq's ally — Kuwait. Using state-of-the-art weaponry, the U.S. Navy blew up an Iranian **oil platform,** destroyed several **small speedboats,** and recklessly shot down an Iranian **passenger airliner,** killing all **290 passengers.**

We had to defend our ship!

*Sure, **what** were they going **to do,** flush their toilets on you?*

After the Iran-Iraq war ended in 1988, Washington was worried that the large army it had helped build in Iraq threatened U.S. domination of the region. Now, it was decided, **something had to be done to disarm Iraq.**

*The sabers were **sharpened.***

In fact, there's evidence that the U.S may have **provoked** and then **lured** Iraq into invading Kuwait, to have a **pretext** for U.S. intervention. The U.S., Saudi Arabia, and Kuwait combined to put **severe economic pressure** on Iraq, which is the reason Iraq began thinking about an invasion in the first place. Then, when Saddam Hussein informed the U.S. about his plans, Washington virtually gave him the **green light**.

"We have **no opinion** on ...your border dispute with Kuwait."

I was hoping you'd say that.

U.S. Embassy

60

U.S. Ambassador April Glaspie, to Saddam Hussein, July 1990. To make sure there was **no confusion**, she added: "James Baker has directed our official spokesmen to emphasize this instruction."

Then, after the invasion, Bush immediately began to prepare for a massive war and **blocked all possibilities for a negotiated solution**. He rejected Iraq's offer to withdraw from Kuwait in exchange for convening a Middle East peace conference (which was mainly a face-saving request).

61

"He's going to get his ass kicked!"

George Bush, December, 1990

Bush knew the conflict could be **settled through negotiations**. But no negotiated settlement would ever have been acceptable. He needed a "**decisive and rapid**" victory. Iraq had to be bombed back to a **pre-industrial age**. Tens of thousands of Iraqi soldiers had to be incinerated. The war had a **message for the world**:

Bush launched the **most intensive bombing campaign** in history using conventional bombs, **cluster bombs** (which rip bodies apart), **napalm** and **phosphorous** bombs (which cling to and burn skin) and **fuel air explosives** (which are like small nuclear bombs). Later, the U.S. used munitions tipped with "**depleted uranium**," which is now suspected as a cause of **cancer** among both Iraqis and U.S. soldiers and **birth defects** among their children.

"What we say goes!"

Boy, we've got some **impressive** weapons!

AMERICA IS NO. 1 — AND DON'T YOU FORGET IT!

Have a nice day! —george

62

Baghdad and Basra were **bombed relentlessly**, killing thousands of civilians.

(63)

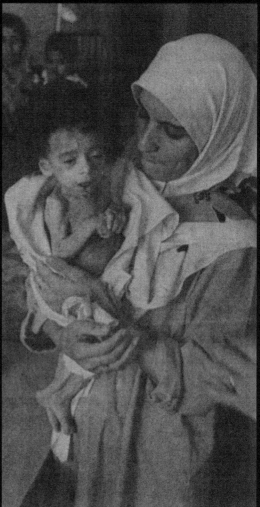

Iraq had already begun to withdraw from Kuwait when Bush launched the ground war. The main aim of the ground offensive was, in fact, **not** to drive the Iraqi troops out of Kuwait, but to **keep them from leaving**. The "**gate was closed**" and tens of thousands of soldiers, who were trying to go home, were **systematically slaughtered**. Elsewhere, U.S. tanks and bulldozers intentionally **buried thousands of soldiers alive** in their trenches in a tactic designed mainly to "destroy Iraqi defenders."

(64)

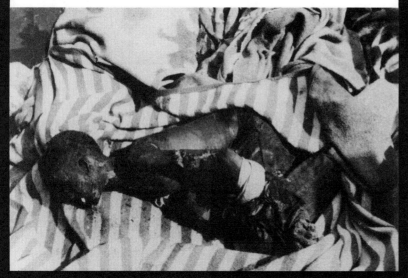

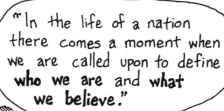

"In the life of a nation there comes a moment when we are called upon to define **who we are** and **what we believe.**"

George H. Bush
January 1991

(65)

(24)

It is estimated that **150,000 Iraqis died** during the Gulf War. But for the people of Iraq, the **tragedy continues** even after the war has ended. Even more people died from **water-borne diseases** that spread because the U.S. systematically destroyed Iraq's **electrical, sewage treatment** and **water treatment** systems. And the U.S. has insisted on maintaining for over a decade the most **severe economic sanctions** regime in history, continuing to strangle the devastated Iraqi economy, with dire consequences for the Iraqi people.

(66)

In 1999, **UNICEF** estimated that infant and child mortality had more than doubled since the war. It largely attributed this sharp reversal in mortality trends to malnutrition and deteriorating health conditions caused by the **war** and **ongoing sanctions**. It estimated that **half a million more children died** as a result. That's 5,200 children a month. ⑥⑦

*That ought to **teach Saddam a lesson** he won't soon forget!*

And the U.S. keeps on bombing Iraq **year after year**.

*Just for **good measure!***

Of course, there were those who **celebrated the war** as a great victory. And indeed it **was** for **some**.

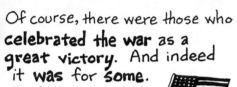
Operation Desert Storm

Who were the winners?

*First, there are the **oil companies**...*

...which reaped **windfall profits** through **speculation** and **price gouging** that drove up gasoline prices. ⑥⑧

Earnings Soar 75% At Exxon

Profits Rise 68.6% At Amoco

Mobil's Profit Jumps 45.6% In Quarter

War Fears Lifted 4th-Quarter Prices; Net at $538 Million

Texaco Net Up 26.5%; Chevron Climbs 17.8%

But **more importantly**, the oil companies **strengthened their grip** on the Middle Eastern oil supply. The war, at least for the time being, preserved the **cozy relationship** between the **oil companies and the royal families** of Kuwait, Saudi Arabia, and the other Gulf emirates (which were all put in place by the British Empire). This cozy relationship has brought **fabulous wealth** to the **owners of the oil companies** and to the **princes and emirs** while the majority of Arab people remain poor. As a result of the Gulf War, **U.S. troops** are now permanently **stationed in Saudi Arabia**, despite **strong opposition** among many Arabs.

EXXON

Emir

⑥⑨

Then there are **the bankers...**

...who are also part of the **partnership** between the Gulf monarchies and the oil companies. Instead of developing the Middle East, the Gulf monarchies have **put the bulk of their money** in the hands of the Western bankers. Some **$900 billion** in Middle Eastern oil profits **fill the vaults** of Citibank, JP Morgan Chase and other banks in the U.S., Europe, and Japan. Therefore, these bankers were also **extremely concerned** about the fate of the Emir of Kuwait and his buddies. ⑦⓪

May **God** save the Emir!

Then there are **the contractors...**

All the big construction contractors, oil service companies, and other major contractors and suppliers all raced to **get their piece** of the **$100 billion** worth of contracts to **rebuild Kuwait.** Giant U.S. corporations, such as Bechtel, Halliburton, AT&T, Motorola and Caterpillar, got the great majority of the contracts.

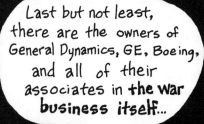

BIG BUCKS CONSTRUCTION INC.

Earthquakes, hurricanes, and industrial accidents are **OK,** but there's nothing like a **good war** for **our bottom line!** ⑦①

Last but not least, there are the owners of General Dynamics, GE, Boeing, and all of their associates in **the war business itself...**

As they watched the **missiles flying** and the **bombs dropping** in the Persian Gulf, the top executives of the big weapons manufacturers were adding up their profits, their brains working like **cash registers gone haywire.**

ch-ching

ch-ching

26

After the Gulf War demonstrated that their weapons can truly **kill on a massive scale**, the arms merchants are busy selling more of them, not only in the halls of **Congress and the Pentagon**, but to generals, bureaucrats, and politicians **around the world.**

U.S. **arms sales** abroad skyrocketed – from $8 billion in 1989 to more than $40 billion in 1991. The U.S. is now selling far more weapons abroad than any country **ever has before.** "Uncle Sam" provides military aid and loan guarantees so that Lockheed-Martin can sell fighter jets even to governments that can't assure their people have enough to eat. (72)

There's **no business** like **war business**...

A **food shortage?** I'm sorry – we're **fresh out** of food financing.

A **bomb shortage?** Now that's **different.** I'm **sure** we can be of **assistance.**

U.S. Aid

U.S. Aid

Of course, there's **no shortage** of public statements about curbing the **international arms race** and the militarization of the Middle East.

"The time has come to try to change the **destructive pattern** of military competition in the [Middle East] and reduce the arms flow to the region."

Sec. of State James Baker, February, 1991 (73)

(74) But while **pious pronouncements** are uttered in Washington, Pentagon representatives have been **busier than ever** selling fighter jets, tanks, helicopters, and cluster bombs to their **favorite customers** in the Middle East, including Israel, the Gulf monarchies, Egypt, and Turkey.

We've got a **real deal** on F-16's this week – buy 100 and **we'll throw in** 1,000 cases of **napalm free!**

FREE **NAPALM OFFER!** We overstocked! Gulf tested! Gulf proven! Kill like you never have before!

Our weapons kill:
• more
• better
• faster

With all of the **wonderful tidings** the Persian Gulf War brought them, it's **no wonder** that many of these major corporations were **prime sponsors** of the "victory parades" that were organized in cities across the country.

On **behalf** of General Dynamics, Exxon, Chase Manhattan Bank, AT&T, McDonnell Douglas, and General Electric, I want to thank you for a job **well done!**

Kosovo, 1999

In the late 1990s, after enduring **years of abuse** at the hands of a Serbian-dominated Yugoslav government, Albanian rebels in Kosovo started a **war for secession.** The U.S. usually does not support minority groups demanding separation. But it **all depends** on whether the U.S. supports the government of the country facing dismemberment. For instance, the U.S. supports **Kurdish separatists** in **Iraq and Iran,** but across the border in **Turkey,** a close ally, Washington has provided tons of arms to **crush the Kurds.** With U.S. help, tens of thousands have been killed.

Our policy is clear— We support people **fighting** for their **freedom** and oppose **terrorist separatists**

75

Because the **Yugoslav strongman,** Slobodan Milosevic, was being less than cooperative with U.S. efforts to extend its influence in Eastern Europe, **breaking up Yugoslavia** was a cause the U.S. could warm up to. The Clinton Administration embraced the Kosovo Liberation Army, despite their **drug dealing, ethnic extremism** and **brutality.** Following established practice, the Administration issued an ultimatum the Yugoslavs **could not possibly accept.**

Here's the deal. First, **NATO** takes over Kosovo. Second, **NATO** has free access to all of Yugoslavia. Third, you help pay for the **NATO-run** government. **Sign here or we bomb you.**

76

The NATO bombing turned an ugly but small-scale Yugoslav counter-insurgency operation into a massive **ethnic cleansing** drive. After the bombing began, Serbian soldiers and militia members began driving hundreds of thousands of Albanians out of the country and killed thousands of others. When the **Albanians** returned under NATO protection, **Serbian** and **Gypsy** residents were driven out and killed. Ultimately, the war served **U.S. political objectives,** while causing tremendous death and suffering on all sides and greatly **aggravating ethnic antagonisms.**

77

Chapter 4
The "War on Terrorism"

After the horrific **September 11 terrorist attacks** on the World Trade Center and the Pentagon, **one question** was so **sensitive** it was seldom seriously addressed by the U.S. news media.

Mom, **why** did they **do it?**

To find out, it makes sense to ask the **prime suspect** himself. As U.S. warplanes began bombing Afghanistan, **Osama bin Laden** released a videotaped message. He **praised** the **September 11 attacks** and called for more attacks on the United States. Then he spelled out his **motivations** quite clearly.

"What America is tasting now is something insignificant compared to what we have tasted for scores of years. Our nation (the Islamic world) has been tasting this **humiliation** and **degradation** for more than **80 years**. Its sons are killed, its **blood is shed**, its sanctuaries are attacked and no one hears and no one heeds. Millions of innocent children are being killed as I speak. They are being killed in **Iraq** without committing any sins.... To **America**, I say only a few words to it and its people. I swear to God, who has elevated the skies without pillars, **neither America nor the people** who live in it will **dream of security** before we live it here in **Palestine** and not before all the **infidel armies leave the land of Muhammad,** peace be upon him." (78)

Osama bin Laden
Oct. 7, 2001

29

Few people anywhere in the world, including the Middle East, support bin Laden's terrorist methods. But most people in the Middle East **share his anger** at the United States. They are angry at the U.S. for supporting **corrupt** and **dictatorial regimes** in the region, for **supporting Israel** at the expense of the Palestinians and for imposing **U.S. dictates** on the Middle East through **military might** and **brutal economic sanctions**.

The Bush Administration immediately instructed U.S. television networks to **"exercise caution"** in airing bin Laden's taped messages. The official reason?

The tapes may contain **secret coded messages** for terrorist operatives

But were **covert messages** the Administration's main concern? Perhaps it was more worried about the impact of bin Laden's **overt message** – that the **September 11** attacks were carried out in **retaliation** for U.S. foreign policy and particularly **U.S. military intervention** in the Middle East.

If Americans realized that U.S. military intervention abroad brought retaliation – causing **death and destruction at home** – we might **think twice** about whether the U.S. should be so **eager to go to war** overseas

The Pentagon has demonstrated time and again that its advanced weaponry can **devastate countries** targeted for attack, **leveling** basic **infrastructure** and **killing thousands**, even hundreds of thousands of people.

It would be **naive** to think there would be **no retaliation**

Over the last several decades the **true costs** of the wars the U.S. has waged overseas have been largely **hidden**. We have had to **pay the military bills** but few Americans have died. The **death** and **destruction** was all **overseas**. That changed on **September 11**.

The **violence** reached the United States

The September 11 attacks, however, were not simply acts of **retribution**. They were also **provocation**. Bin Laden expected the U.S. to respond with **massive violence**, knowing this would bring him **new recruits**. Ultimately, he hoped to win the majority of the Muslim world to support his **holy war on the U.S.**

More **martyrs**, more **recruits**.

The Bush Administration responded according to **bin Laden's script**. George W. Bush declared a **"War on Terrorism,"** using "good vs. evil" rhetoric that mirrored bin Laden's. Bush and his advisors were ready, **even eager**, for the war bin Laden wanted. They saw the September 11 attacks as a **grand opportunity** to boost military spending and demonstrate U.S. military power.

"This will be a monumental struggle of **good versus evil**... This **crusade**, this **war on terrorism**, is going to take a while"

G.W. Bush, Sept. 12 and 16, 2001

Bush's **"War on Terrorism"** began with U.S. warplanes **bombing Afghanistan**. The Bush Administration refused to negotiate or consider any **alternatives to war**. When the Afghan government asked for evidence against bin Laden, a reasonable request that might have made it possible to cooperate with the U.S., Bush replied:

I said - **no negotiations!** Cough up bin Laden now or **die** along with him!

Relatives prepare the bodies of four small children for burial after a U.S. airstrike. Kabul, October 2001.

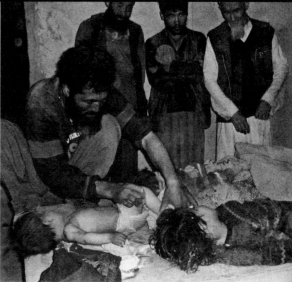

The people of Afghanistan **suffered the consequences**. **U.S. bombing** killed many civilians and the war cut off relief supplies to millions already **facing starvation**. The total number of deaths will never be known, but it's likely there will be many times more **civilian deaths** in Afghanistan than in the World Trade Center.

As warplanes of the world's **richest and most powerful** country bombed people in one of the **poorest and most miserable** countries on earth, the streets of cities throughout the Muslim world filled with **angry demonstrations**. Not only religious radicals were angry. Almost everybody in the Muslim world **opposed the war**.

USA
THE REAL TERRORIST

The war **added fuel** to simmering anti-American sentiments in the Middle East. Bombing Muslim countries and sending U.S. troops into this volatile region will only inspire more hatred for the United States and **more terrorist attacks** on Americans. Bush surely knows this, yet he decided to go ahead and **place us in greater danger** anyway.

We **never said** this war was not going to have **costs!**

The War on Terrorism **cannot possibly end terrorism**. Even if bin Laden is killed, **new converts will rally** to join his war to drive the U.S. out of the Middle East. The **spiral of violence** is escalating dangerously.

And the warmakers on both sides are **itching to escalate!**

The self-righteous "**good vs. evil**" rhetoric of the War on Terrorism sharpens ironies that have long shadowed U.S. pronouncements against **state-sponsored terrorism**. President Bush, for instance, promises to scour the globe in search of **states** that **harbor terrorists**.

He could start in the **State of Florida**

What do you mean?

For over forty years, **Miami** has served as the base of operations for well-financed groups of **Cuban exiles** that have carried out violent **terrorist attacks on Cuba**.

Most recently, they **bombed** a number of Havana tourist spots in 1997, killing an Italian tourist, and they tried to **assassinate** Fidel Castro in Panama in 2000.

32

It would not be difficult for the government to find evidence involving these terrorist organizations because the **CIA** and the **Pentagon trained** many of their **members**. Take, for instance, **Luis Posada Carriles** and **Orlando Bosch**, suspected masterminds of the **bombing** of a **Cuban passenger airliner** that claimed the lives of **73 people**.

(81)

"All of Castro's planes are **warplanes**"

Orlando Bosch, 1987, defending the bombing of the civilian Cuban plane

Before Posada Carriles could be tried for the airline bombing, he **escaped** from a **prison** in Venezuela and found a job **supplying arms** to the CIA-backed **Nicaraguan contras**.

My **experience** in the **CIA** gave me the **right credentials** for the job

(82)

Posada's accomplice, Orlando Bosch, has long been **protected from extradition** by the U.S. goverment. Although Bosch was convicted of carrying out a **bazooka attack** on a ship in **Miami harbor**, President Bush's father, George H., at the urging of his brother, Jeb, prevented his expulsion from the country. He signed an **executive pardon** providing Bosch with **safe haven** in Florida. Bosch promised he would...

(83)

"Rejoin the **struggle!**"

(84)

Hold on! Let me set the record straight. I **pardon only freedom fighters**, not terrorists!

If the younger Bush were serious about going after **all** states that **harbor terrorists**, he might issue his **next ultimatum** to **his brother**, the governor of Florida.

Listen Jeb, you're going to have to **cough up** the terrorists or we start **bombing Miami** tomorrow!

Posada, Bosch and their friends are **only a few** of the violent characters whose activities have been sponsored by the CIA. Many of the CIA's "**covert operations**" — bombings, **assassinations, sabotage, paramilitary massacres** — are terrorism by any definition. Many of the shadowy figures involved in these activities are still working with the CIA around the world. But others — including **Osama bin Laden** — have **turned on their former partners**.

It's **too bad**. They made such a **good team**.

(85)

Even Congressional opposition to the far-fetched **"missile defense program"** collapsed.

Beep Beep

Missile defense, like the "War on Terrorism," **promises to protect Americans** from danger while actually creating a much **more dangerous world**. If other countries think there is any chance the U.S. could block their missiles, they will feel **vulnerable** to U.S. attack. China has already promised to build more and better missiles which could overwhelm the U.S. "missile shield." This will spur a **nuclear arms race in Asia**.

If **China** builds more nuclear missiles, then **India** will. If India does, then **Pakistan** will. If Pakistan...

(87)

In 1972, the U.S. and the U.S.S.R. signed the **ABM Treaty** to try to avoid this kind of arms race. In order to pursue missile defense, the U.S. **unilaterally scrapped** the treaty. But that didn't bother missile defense proponents.

In this spirit, while the Pentagon has reduced its arsenal of vulnerable land-based missiles, it continues to spend billions to build more **submarine-based nuclear missiles**. And Congress has **rejected** the nuclear **test ban treaty**, which has been signed by 164 countries.

(88)

Hey, the world's changed. **We can win an arms race** with anyone!

The U.S. is keeping enough nuclear firepower to **wipe out** most of **humanity**.

Just to be safe!

(36)

As potential nuclear targets in Russia have declined, the Pentagon has been retargeting its missiles at **"every reasonable adversary."**

Which makes other countries feel like they better **hurry up** and get nuclear weapons themselves

(89)

In the post-Cold War world order, the U.S. does not seem to want to be bound by any arms treaties. It **refuses to sign** a new protocol to the 1972 biological weapons treaty because it would require **international inspections** of its **biological weapons research facilities**, where it is creating **deadly new strains** including highly lethal **powdered anthrax.** U.S. officials say they are only creating germ weapons in order to study how to defend against them.

Of course, we would **never** use them **ourselves!**

(90)

But can other countries **trust** a government that bombed Hiroshima and Nagasaki and actually developed plans to use **smallpox** and other biological weapons against **Vietnam** and **Cuba?**

Would you?

(91)

And U.S. **"weaponized germs"** not only represent a threat to people in other countries.

What if some of the Pentagon's powdered anthrax got into the hands of **some fanatic here** in the United States?

During the Cold War the U.S. had a serious military competitor in the Soviet Union. Today the U.S. maintains a huge war machine despite the **lack of any serious competition.** The U.S. military budget is now larger than the next 25 biggest spenders **put together!** It makes up a full **36%** of **total global military spending.**

United States $396 billion

Annual Military Expenditures
The world's four biggest spenders

Russia $60 billion

China $42 billion

Japan $40 billion

— 400

— 300

Billions of U.S. Dollars

Being the **world cop** and all, we do have certain responsibilities!

(92)

If we add up the **current Pentagon budget**, the **nuclear weapons** budget of the **Energy Department**, the military portion of the **NASA** budget, foreign **military aid**, **veterans' benefits**, **interest payments** on debt incurred by past military spending and other military-related expenses, the U.S. spends over $**776 billion a year** to feed its **addiction to war**. ⑨⑥

That's more than a **million** dollars a **minute!**

This **costs you plenty**. An **average American household** "contributes" over $**4,400** in taxes every year to the cause of building up the world's most powerful military. ⑨⑦

Now I know why we can't ever seem to make ends meet!

Mom- could we get...

If you need anything else, just **give a holler!**

Because Congress is **so generous** to the **Pentagon**...

Social programs get **short-changed**.

That's all we can afford - we can't **bust the budget**, you know.

Bridges, roads, sewers, and water systems are **crumbling** because the government fails to provide the money needed to maintain them.

Bus fares are rising and **service** is being **slashed** as the Federal Government has eliminated financial support for mass transit operating costs.

⑨⑧

⑨⑨

Schools are **run-down** and over-crowded. In some inner-city high schools, 80% of the students drop out. More than a fifth of all adults **can't read** a job application or a street sign. Yet federal education funding per student has declined substantially over the last two decades.

We believe in **bake** sale financing.

Skyrocketing prices are causing a **crisis in health care.** **43 million** people have **no insurance** and millions more have inadequate insurance. More and more people don't get the medical care they need because they can't afford it. Yet **public hospitals are being closed** and the government has failed to enact any serious health care reform.

INSURED PATIENTS →

← UNINSURED PATIENTS

EXIT

Reception

Mom, it **hurts!**

One-fifth of all **expectant mothers** do not receive **pre-natal care.** This is one reason the U.S. has the highest infant mortality rate in the developed world (twice as high as Japan's). **Every 50 minutes,** a child in the U.S. dies as a result of **poverty or hunger.** Yet Congress has been exceedingly stingy in funding maternal and child health programs.

I just **love** babies!

Why don't you put your **money** where your **mouth** is, mister?

Yuck!

Vote for Me!

With **rents rising** and **wages falling,** millions of families are living on the verge of eviction. Millions of people end up **living on the streets.** Yet when it comes to funding for housing and homelessness, most of Washington seems to have adopted Reagan's attitude.

Those people **want** to live on the streets!

40

Drug addiction and alcoholism are crippling millions of people, and devastating families and whole communities. Yet there are not enough public treatment centers to handle **even a fraction** of those seeking help, and many centers are **closing their doors** for lack of funding.

There's just **no money!**

Oh yeah?

Somehow you come up with billions of dollars a year to operate **12 aircraft carrier battle groups!**

With the $1,000,000,000 it takes to maintain just one of those aircraft carriers for a year, you could build **17,000 homes** for 67,000 people

...or you could provide **free prenatal care** for 1,600,000 expectant mothers, saving thousands of babies

(105)

(104)

...or enroll 384,000 more kids in the **Head Start** preschool program this year

...or provide intensive **drug or alcohol treatment** for 333,000 people

(106)

(107)

41

... or give 500,000 malnourished children in this country **three meals a day** for a year

...or you could put a down payment on a **brand new** aircraft carrier!

U.S.S. Ronald Reagan

108

Which is **exactly** what they are doing – building a new aircraft carrier!

The government can find **hundreds of billions** for new aircraft carriers and other military hardware...

But they **say** they **can't find** the money to deal with the pressing **problems** we face!

109

The **price of militarism** includes more than high taxes and poor social services. Building nuclear weapons, for instance, has probably been the **biggest environmental disaster** this country has ever seen. More than 100 nuclear weapons plants owned by the Energy Department have been **spewing radioactive waste** into the air, dumping it in rivers, and leaking it into the soil and groundwater for decades.

All **under the cover** of government secrecy

RESTRICTED AREA
NATIONAL SECURITY
KEEP YOUR NOSE OUT

The administrators who run the nuclear weapons plants have **knowingly** subjected the people who work in them and the people who live near them to **deadly radioactive contamination** – without telling them a word about it.

The government now estimates it will take **25,000 workers** at least **30 years** to clean up the mess at these plants – at a cost of **$300 billion** or more.

And guess who's **paying the bill**!

Beep Beep

110

What's more, nuclear weapons tests have spread deadly **plutonium** across large tracts of the Southwest and the South Pacific. Many of the 458,000 U.S. soldiers who participated in the atomic testing program are now **dying of cancer**.

Don't worry, kid. It's perfectly safe. Just wear these **goggles!**

?

US

U.S. ARMY   PVT. GRUNT

111

But they're not the only ones. **High cancer rates** plague the general population in the testing areas. One study estimated that by the end of this century nuclear testing worldwide will have caused **430,000 people** to die of cancer.

112

And plutonium remains **highly radioactive** for hundreds of thousands of years.

43

Meanwhile, at military bases around the country they've been **dumping hundreds of thousands of tons of toxic wastes**, including chemical warfare agents, napalm, explosives, PCB's, and heavy metals, creating malignant lagoons and **contaminating the groundwater** of surrounding communities.

There are 11,000 military dump sites that need to be cleaned up. The estimated cost — **$100 to $200 billion**.

(113)

I say let's fence 'em all off and call them **national security sacrifice zones.**

DANGE
KEEP OU
TOXIC W

He's serious—that's what some people are proposing.

Nearly everyone in this country pays a high price for militarism. But those among us who have paid the **highest price** are the **millions of soldiers** who have been sent overseas to fight.

More than **100,000 U.S. soldiers and sailors have died** in foreign wars since U.S. troops were sent to Korea in 1950.

(114)

Hundreds of thousands more have been wounded, many **disabled for life.** Many Gulf War veterans are suffering the effects of **"Gulf War Syndrome."**

Those who survive continue to be **haunted by the wars** they fought in. Half a million **veterans** of the Vietnam War suffer from post-traumatic stress disorder - caused by memories of the horrors of the war. The number of Vietnam vets who have **killed themselves** since the war is greater than the number of U.S. soldiers who died in the war. (115)

Hundreds of thousands of military veterans have ended up living on the streets. (116)

And the **killing goes on**, even between wars.

Every year, more than a thousand U.S. soldiers and sailors are killed in **military accidents**. They are burned to death in fires at sea, crushed by tanks, and blown up by practice artillery fire.

BOOM

U.S. NAVY

They break their necks jumping out of planes in high wind, and crash in **unsafe helicopters**. (117)

SNAP

?!

These are all victims of Washington's **addiction to militarism**. And there are more victims...

Every year, hundreds of active-duty soldiers and sailors **commit suicide**.

US ARMY   PVT. JONE

Of course, nobody is **born** with a desire to be **humiliated and treated like a "grunt"**, much less to be killed. So **indoctrination** into the culture of militarism starts early.

Bang! Bang! You're dead!

(45)

Television, movies, video games, and toy stores all make **killing** seem not only glorious, but **fun**.

High school principals lock the doors and hire armed guards, supposedly to protect the kids from **drug dealers, pimps, and other dangerous characters**. But they roll out the red carpet for the **most dangerous characters of all** – the **military recruiters**.

The recruiters, who are not quite as honest as used car salesmen, come armed with **slick brochures and glossy promises**.

By the time the recruits find out what **military life** is really all about, they're **trapped**.

The ones who end up on the **front lines** are usually kids who can't find a job or pay for college. Almost all of them are from **working-class families**, and a disproportionate number are African Americans, Mexican Americans, Puerto Ricans, Native Americans, and other national minorities. As a result, it's mostly the poor who **die on the battlefield**.

The **greatest injustice** is that the people who start the wars are not the ones who fight and die.

My daddy told me I could **serve my country** better by going to **law school!**

Maria Cotto spoke out against this injustice. **Her brother** was killed in the Persian Gulf War:

" I saw them on television saying they were spending billions on this. I saw them on **Wall Street** and they were cheering. It was sick, they were **cheering like it was a game...**"

" Don't they know it means people will die? Not **them**. Not **their** families. Not **their** kids. People like my brother."

⑪⑨

Ismael Cotto, 27 years old, Bronx, New York. Killed in Saudi Arabia, Jan. 1991

It's the **working people** of this country who pay the price of foreign wars— **in blood and in taxes.**

Others reap the benefits

For **most** people, the huge Pentagon budget means **less money** in their pockets.

IRS

PENTAGON

But for **some** people, just the **opposite** is true.

War Profits

Over 100,000 companies **feed** at the **Pentagon trough**. But the **big money** goes to a handful of huge corporations.

Outa the way! I was here first!

1999 Pentagon Contracts

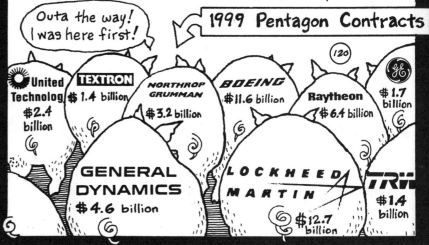

United Technolog $2.4 billion

TEXTRON $1.4 billion

NORTHROP GRUMMAN $3.2 billion

BOEING $11.6 billion

Raytheon $6.4 billion

GE $1.7 billion

GENERAL DYNAMICS $4.6 billion

LOCKHEED MARTIN $12.7 billion

TRW $1.4 billion

The families that own these corporations owe their wealth to the **Pentagon's generosity** with your tax money. So they don't mind **sharing a little** with their friends and benefactors in Washington.

Here's to the Pentagon – the only place you can sell a 13¢ bolt for $2043!

Dick Cheney, George W. Bush's Vice-President and chief advisor is one of the politicians who has made a very **profitable career** out of promoting the **military-industrial complex**. After presiding over the Gulf War as Defense Secretary under George W.'s father, Cheney was named CEO of Halliburton, Inc. As the world's biggest oil services firm with a **huge stake** in the Middle East, Halliburton was a major beneficiary of the Gulf War. It is also a big military contractor, **raking in billions** for building military bases and providing battlefield services. Under Cheney, Halliburton's government contracts **increased sharply**.

I knew we were getting the **right guy** for the job!

Cheney was **rewarded handsomely**, pocketing millions in salary and stock options every year. He ended up as Halliburton's largest individual stockholder, with a $45 million stake. (123)

I **earned** every penny of it!

Cheney was also invited to serve on the boards of two other huge war contractors, TRW and EDS. His wife, Lynn, joined the board of Lockheed-Martin. After Cheney returned to the White House in 2001, Lockheed-Martin was awarded the **biggest plum** in the history of war contracts — a deal to manufacture the next generation of fighter jets worth hundreds of billions of dollars. It's no wonder the Cheneys are among the most **avid champions** of the "War on Terrorism."

We're just doing our **patriotic duty!**

(124)

In the front lines of the **pro-war crowd** you will find an assortment of bankers, corporate executives, politicians and generals. If you ask them why they are so fond of going to war they will give you **noble** and **selfless reasons**.

Democracy.   Freedom.   Justice.   Peace.

But what **really motivates** them to go to war are **somewhat less lofty** aims:

Money!   Markets!   Natural resources!   Power!

Chapter 6
Militarism and the Media

For some people, **war** means **handsome profits** and overseas investment opportunities.

But for most people, war means **higher taxes** and **body bags**.

It's not surprising, therefore, that most people are **less enthusiastic** about going to war than the war profiteers are.

Here.

Uhh... lemme **think** about it.

Because people are often **reluctant** to support wars half way around the world, the government and it's spokespeople have always had to go to **great lengths** to convince people to go along with these wars. They wrap them up in **red, white and blue** and present them to the people as their **patriotic duty.**

?

TIC TIC

They paint monstrous pictures of the **enemy of the hour.**

Reliable sources reported today that _____ eats **babies for dinner.**

Fill in the blank.

Since the days of William Randolph Hearst, the **pro-war message** has been delivered to the people by the **news media**.

Typical Hearst journalism, 1917

But it was after World War II that the press, the radio networks, and the fledgling television industry became **fully integrated** into the **newly emerging military-industrial complex.**

With the **"Cold War"** getting under way, this complex had its work cut out for it. Charles Wilson, Chairman of the Board of **General Electric** (whom Truman had just appointed to head the **Office of Defense Mobilization**), spelled out what this work was in a speech to the Newspaper Publishers Association in 1950:

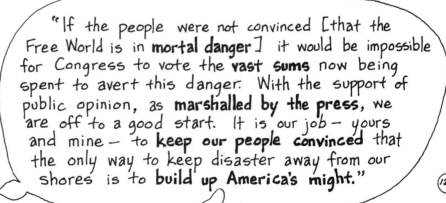

"If the people were not convinced [that the Free World is in **mortal danger**] it would be impossible for Congress to vote the **vast sums** now being spent to avert this danger. With the support of public opinion, as **marshalled by the press**, we are off to a good start. It is our job — yours and mine — to **keep our people convinced** that the only way to keep disaster away from our shores is to **build up America's might.**"

(125)

Charles Wilson and his cronies at GE were, of course, **very eager** to see a massive military build up.

GE had **major investments** around the world, which they expected the Pentagon to protect. It also was, and is, **a charter member** of the military-industrial complex.

A member in good standing, I might add!

GE is the country's third-largest military contractor, **raking in billions** of dollars every year. It produces parts for every nuclear weapon in the U.S. arsenal, makes jet engines for military aircraft, and creates all kinds of **profitable electronic gadgets** for the Pentagon. It's also the company that secretly released **millions of curies** of deadly radiation from the Hanford nuclear weapons facility in Washington state and produced **faulty nuclear power plants** that dot the U.S. countryside.

"We bring good things to life!"

From Wilson's time, GE has been very concerned with making use of the media. In 1954 it hired a **floundering actor** named Ronald Reagan to be its **corporate spokesman**. It furnished Ron and Nancy with an all-electric house, and Ron with his own TV show called **"GE Theater."**

It also furnished Reagan with **"The Speech,"** GE's political message for America, and sent him around the country to deliver it. He's been delivering variations of "The Speech" **ever since**.

(126)

Meanwhile, GE was busy **buying up** TV and radio stations across the country.

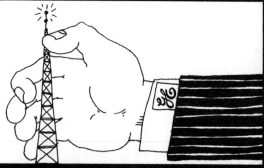

Then, in 1986, GE bought **its own TV network — NBC**

Good evening, I'm **Tom Brokaw** and this is the NBC Nightly News.

127

Charles Wilson would be **pleased** with NBC's programming. The network is very good at marshalling public opinion along just the lines he suggested. And NBC is not alone. You get just about **the same message** no matter what channel you turn to.

Our game plan is right on schedule...

Our game plan is right on schedule...

Our game plan is right on schedule...

After the Persian Gulf War, one of the Bush Administration's top war planners spoke to a group of **prominent journalists** and thanked them for their help.

"[Television was] our **chief tool** in selling our policy."

Richard Hass, National Security Council, 1991

128

It sure was. We were treated to live 24-hour war coverage, **sponsored by** Exxon and General Electric and **cleared by** the Pentagon.

Just **how many lives** can these new high-tech weapons **save,** Colonel?

When it comes to **war**, the networks discard all **pretenses** of objectivity.

Bomb 'em back! Bomb 'em back! **Wwwway** back!

Lawrence Grossman, who was in charge of **PBS** and **NBC News** for many years, described the role of the press this way:

"The job of the President is to set the agenda and the job of the press is to **follow the agenda** that the leadership sets." (129)

Why do all the networks sound the same? Why are they all **consumed by war fever** every time the White House decides to send troops oversees?

Maybe it's got something to do with **who controls them**

The television news media are owned by some of the largest corporations in the country. NBC, as we have seen, is owned by GE, CBS is owned by Viacom, ABC is owned by Disney, and CNN is owned by AOL Time Warner. The members of the boards of directors of these powerful corporations also sit on the boards of **weapons manufaturers** and other companies with **vested interests** around the world such as Sun Microsystems, EDS, Lucent Technologies, Prudential, etc.

Our networks tell you everything you **need to know**

XEROX JPMorganChase (130) CHRYSLER Marriott CITIBANK®

Most of the news available to us — about war and peace and everything else — is **filtered through the perspective** of the corporate news media. The government and the news media obviously have a **powerful influence** on public opinion.

But their influence is not as complete as they **might hope**.

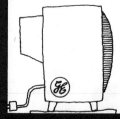

Everyone is rallying behind the President.

Hmmm...Oo

Chapter 7
Resisting Militarism

In fact, there's been **strong opposition** to foreign military adventures since the Mexican-American and Spanish-American wars of the last century. The **anti-war movement** grew especially strong during the war to conquer the Philippines.

"I have seen that we do not intend to free but to **subjugate** the Philippines. And so I am an **anti-imperialist**. I am opposed to having the **eagle put its talons on any other land**... I have a strong aversion to sending our bright boys out there to fight with a **disgraced musket** under a **polluted flag.**"

Mark Twain,
Vice President,
Anti-Imperialist League,
1900

(131)

Let's go back to Charles Wilson's era, when he and the media were **mobilizing support** for the **Korean War.** At first they were very successful. But despite their impressive efforts, the support **didn't last long.** After the body bags started coming home, the majority of people turned against the war.

I want my son back home! Now.

The government and the media once again did their best to whip up support for the war in Vietnam. But as the **war escalated,** the greatest anti-war movement in U.S. history arose. At first, the opposition was **small but determined.**

BRING OUR MEN HOME

But opposition **grew by leaps and bounds** as people began to learn what was going on in Vietnam. By 1969 there were 750,000 people **marching on Washington,** and millions more marching in cities across the country.

In May 1970, after police and National Guard troops **fired on anti-war demonstrations,** killing four students at Kent State in Ohio and two students at Jackson State in Mississippi, students at 400 universities across the country went on strike — the **first general student strike** in U.S. history. (132)

When police shot and killed three people during the **Chicano Moratorium** against the war in August 1971, a rebellion raged through East Los Angeles for three days. (133)

Resistance to the war took many forms. People **refused to pay war taxes.**

Paycheck

People burned their draft cards.

Hell no, we won't go!

SELECTIVE SERVICE

The most famous **draft resister** was Muhammad Ali.

> I won't serve in a **white man's war!**

People **blocked the path of trains** hauling troops and munitions bound for the war.

STOP THE WAR!

STOP THE TRAIN

14,000 people were arrested when they moved to **shut down Washington, D.C.,** for three days in 1971.

> It was the largest mass arrest in U.S. history!

(134)

Even more serious for the Pentagon, **discipline was breaking down** among the troops in Vietnam. The soldiers saw no reason to fight, and they wouldn't. By the end of the '60s, a **virtual civil war** simmered between soldiers and officers. A U.S. military expert warned the Pentagon about the state of its army:

(135) (136)

> " [By] every conceivable indicator, our army that now remains in Vietnam is in a state **approaching collapse,** with individual units avoiding or having **refused combat, murdering their officers** and non-commissioned officers, drug-ridden and dispirited where not **near mutinous.**"

Col. Robert Heinl, U.S.M.C. retired, 1971

Record numbers of soldiers and sailors **deserted or went AWOL.** Organized resistance was developing among the troops. Hundreds of **underground G.I. newspapers** were springing up at bases around the U.S. and around the world. Contingents of soldiers and sailors were marching at the head of anti-war demonstrations.

Soldiers coming home from Vietnam were telling the country about the **horrors of the war** and they were organizing to stop it. In April 1971, more than a thousand **Vietnam veterans** gathered at the Capitol Building in Washington and **threw back the medals** they had received in the war.

(137)

By the end of the decade, the majority of the people were **against the war.**

The **anti-war movement**, together with the **struggles** waged by African Americans, Latinos, Native Americans, and other oppressed peoples in the U.S., and the women's liberation movement were opening people's eyes to **a whole system of injustice.**

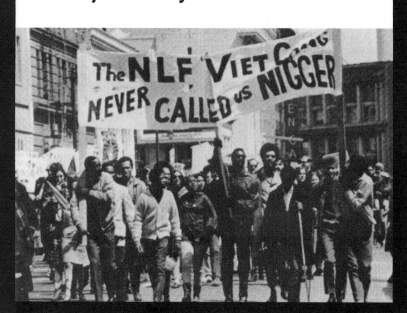

The NLF, VIET CONG NEVER CALLED us NIGGER

The growing opposition to the war played an important role in convincing the government that it **had to pull out** of Vietnam.

"The **weakest chink in our armor** is American public opinion. Our people won't stand firm in the face of heavy losses, and they can **bring down the government.**"

President Lyndon Johnson, 1968

(138)

As a result of the Vietnam War, a broad anti-militarist sentiment developed among the American people, which was derisively called the **"Vietnam Syndrome"** in official circles.

Don't talk about that **dreadful disease!**

When George H. sent troops to the Persian Gulf, people were **very apprehensive**. The majority did not want to go to war. A powerful anti-war movement grew more quickly than ever before in U.S. history.

Soon the **streets were filled** with demonstrations.

After the bombs started dropping, the **pro-war media blitz** convinced many people that they shouldn't oppose the war because they might be endangering U.S. troops.

The media forgot to mention that it was Bush who **put us in danger** in the first place.

And that the best way to get us out of danger is to **get us out of here!**

Immediately after the war began, hundreds of thousands of people marched in San Francisco and Washington, D.C.

George the Elder knew he had to finish the war quickly and with few U.S. casualties or the people would **turn against it**. When Iraq chose to withdraw rather than fight and the war ended with a **one-sided slaughter**, Bush was **euphoric**.

" **By God,** we've kicked the **Vietnam Syndrome** once and for all!"

George H., February 1991

The government tried to organize **pro-war rallies** while the bombs were falling, but only a few people showed up.

Turn Baghdad into a **parking lot!**

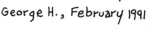

OPERATION DESERT STORM

59

139

George W. Bush seems to be out to test his father's proposition. He has promised us a **long** and **bloody** War on Terrorism with lots of casualties. The war in **Afghanistan**, he has declared, is *"just the beginning of the war against terror."*
(140)

*"There's a **variety of theaters**. So long as anybody's **terrorizing** established governments, there **needs to be a war**."*

George W. Bush
October 17, 2001

(141)

If Bush is serious, we may be facing an **endless war**. Terrorist tactics have been around as long as war and are unlikely to disappear in our lifetimes. Maybe Bush's language is simply rhetorical excess. But it's also possible he and his advisors envision an era of **uninterrupted warfare**, in which one country after another will be **targeted for bombing**.

Which will **make us** the **targets** of more retaliation!

It seems that Dick Cheney, for one, is ready for this. Emerging from his **secret bunker**, he warned that the "War on Terrorism" would go on for a long time.

(142)

*"It may **never end**. At least not in our lifetime"*

CHENEY

Cheney, Oct. 2001

As part of this endless war, he declared, we have to be prepared for **ongoing terrorist attacks**.

(143)

*"For the first time in our history we will probably suffer **more casualties** here **at home** than will our troops overseas"*

Cheney, Oct. 2001

This means, he said, that we have to get used to invasive security measures and **sacrifice civil liberties**.

*"We're going to have to take steps... that'll become a permanent part of our **way of life**"*

Cheney, Oct. 2001

(144)

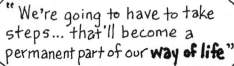

After **September 11**, Americans were stunned by the **horror** of the terrorist attacks. Bush's **bellicose** words resonated among many. But as the **"War on Terrorism"** goes on, will this initial support **last** longer than it did during the Korean and Vietnam Wars? Even Bush worries that it won't.

*"People are going to **get tired** of the War on Terrorism"*

George W. Bush, October 17, 2001

(145)

Bush and Cheney offer us a **very grim** vision of the future — War, which will provoke more terrorist attacks, which will be met with more war, which will inspire more terrorism. **Sensible people** will not be willingly dragged down this **path of violence and retaliation**.

Thousands march to protest U.S. war plans for Afghanistan, Washington, D.C., Sept. 2001

The "War on Terrorism" continues an **inglorious history** of militarism. **Militarism** is the bloody attendant of **empire**. Do we really want to allow this tradition to continue?

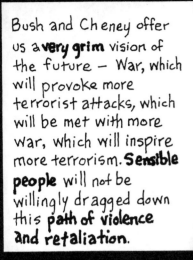

As they whip up **war fever** and ask you to put your life on the line, whether in a **bomber** in the skies over the Middle East or as a potential **bomb victim** in New York, ask yourself...

What is this **addiction to war** doing to the people of the U.S. and the world?

How much does it **cost**?

MILLION $ A MINUTE

The Next Chapter
Do Something About It!

Here are **a few groups** that are trying to figure that out...

We've only been able to include in this list a small number of the many groups conducting anti-militarist education and organizing anti-war activities in the U.S. The movement is growing rapidly and is very diverse. Some of the most vibrant organizations are fledging, local, sectional, and idiosyncratic (and didn't make it on this list). More organizations are listed on Frank Dorrel's website (www.addictedtowar.com). We encourage you to contact groups whose activities are most closely aligned with your own concerns, beliefs, and talents.

American Friends Service Committee

1501 Cherry Street, Philadelphia, PA 19102
Tel: 215-241-7000; Fax: 215-241-7177
Email: afscinfo@afsc.org
Website: www.afsc.org

Founded in 1917, AFSC is a Quaker organization that includes people of various faiths committed to humanitarian service. Our work is based on the belief in the worth of every person and faith in the power of love to overcome violence and injustice. Programs in the U.S., Africa, Asia, Europe, Latin America, and the Middle East focus on issues related to economic and social justice, youth, peace-building and demilitarization.

Central Committee of Conscientious Objectors

1515 Cherry Street, Philadelphia, PA 19102
Tel: 215-563-8787; Toll Free: 1-800-NOJROTC
G.I Rights Hotline: 1-800-394-9544
Website: www.objector.org

The CCCO promotes individual and collective resistance to war and preparations for war. It has been active since 1948, helping people seek discharge from active military service on grounds of conscientious objection, providing information and assistance to those faced with a military draft, enlistment obligations, and registration.

Democracy Now! with Amy Goodman

87 Lafayette, New York, NY 10013
Tel: 212-431-9272
Email: mail@democracynow.org
Website: www.democracynow.org

Democracy Now! is a national radio and TV show committed to bringing the voices of the marginalized to the airwaves to discuss global and local issues, including militarism. Democracy Now! is broadcast on the Pacifica radio network (KPFA, 94.1 FM, Berkeley; KPFK, 90.7 FM, Los Angeles; KPFT, 90.1 FM, Houston; WBAI, 99.5 FM, New York; WPFW, 89.3 FM, Washington, DC) and on other community radio stations, Free Speech TV (Dish Network Channel 9415), and public access television stations.

Fellowship of Reconciliation

P.O. Box 271, Nyack, NY 10960
Tel: 845-358-4601; Fax: 845-358-4924
Email: info@forusa.org; Website: www.forusa.org

FOR seeks to replace violence, war, racism, and economic injustice with nonviolence, peace, and justice. We are an interfaith organization committed to active nonviolence as a transforming way of life and as a means of radical change. We educate, train, build coalitions, and engage in nonviolent, compassionate actions.

Global Peace Campaign

1047 Naka, Kamogawa, Chiba, Japan 296-0111
Tel: 81-470-97-1011; Fax: 81-470-97-1215
Email: yumik@awa.or.jp
Website: www.peace2001.org

Founded after the September 11 attacks, GPC supports anti-war education in the United States and Japan. Among its projects have been anti-war billboards and peace ads in major newspapers.

Global Exchange

2017 Mission Street #303
San Francisco, CA 94110
Tel: 415-255-7296; Fax: 415-255-7498
Website: www.globalexchange.org

Global Exchange is a not-for-profit international human rights organization. Through diverse programs including reality tours to dozens of countries, fair trade stores, corporate accountability campaigns, anti-war work, green economy promotion, we seek to accelerate the paradigm shift from money values and violence to life values and nonviolence.

International Action Center

39 W. 14th St. # 206, New York, NY 10011
Tel: 212-633-6646; Fax: 212-633-2889
Email: iacenter@iacenter.org
Website: www.iacenter.org

Founded by Ramsey Clark, former U.S. Attorney General, the IAC provides information and organizes resistance to U.S. militarism, war, and corporate greed, linking these issues with struggles against domestic racism and oppression.

Not in Our Name

Tel: 212-969-8058
Email: info@notinourname.net
Website: www.notinourname.net

NION is a creative coalition of anti-war activists that has grown into one of the most formidable resistance efforts since the Vietnam War. The NION Pledge of Resistance was created to inspire protest and show solidarity with the people of nations harmed by U.S. militarism.

True Majority

PO Box 1976, Old Chelsea Station,
New York, NY 10113-1976
Tel: 212-243-3416
Website: www.truemajority.com

TM is a free service led by Ben Cohen, founder of Ben and Jerry's. We monitor Congress on issues of social justice and environmental sustainability. Among our goals are to ease the nuclear nightmare, renounce the militarization of space, and make globalization work for, not against, working people. When your voice needs to be heard you get an e-mail alert; by clicking reply you send a fax to your congressperson.

Office of the Americas

8124 W. 3rd Street, Suite 202
Los Angeles, CA 90048-4309
Phone: 323-852-9808;
Email: ooa@igc.org
Website: www.officeoftheamericas.org

The OOA is a non-profit corporation dedicated to furthering the cause of justice and peace through broad-based education including delegations, participation in television, radio, and print media, and presentations to university and high school classes and civic and religious organizations.

Peace Action

1819 H. Street NW, Suite #420 and #425,
Washington, DC 20006
Phone: 202-862-9740; Fax: 202-862-9762
Website: www.peace-action.org

Peace Action (formerly SANE/Freeze) works to achieve the abolition of nuclear weapons, the development of a peace-oriented economy, and an end to the international weapons trade. We promote non-military solutions to international conflicts.

School of the Americas Watch

PO Box 4566, Washington DC 20017
Tel: 202-234-3440; Fax: 202-636-4505
Website: www.soaw.org

SOAW works in solidarity with the people of Latin America to change oppressive U.S. foreign policies. In particular, we work to close the School of the Americas/Western Hemisphere Institute for Security Cooperation, where the Pentagon trains Latin American military officers in methods of repression and torture.

Teaching for Change

PO Box 73038; Washington, DC 20056
Toll Free: 1-800-763-9131
Tel: 202-588-7204; Fax: 202-238-0109
Email: tfe@teachingforchange.org
Website: www.teachingforchange.org

Teaching for Change promotes social and economic justice through public education. We provide vital services and resources in the DC Metro area and nationally for K-12 teachers, parents and teacher educators, through our catalog, training and other support.

Veterans for Peace

438 N. Skinker
St. Louis, MO. 63130
Tel: 314-725-6005
Email: vfp@igc.org
Website: www.veteransforpeace.org

VFP is an organization of men and women who served in the military and who work toward abolishing war through promoting alternatives to war. VFP is dedicated to educating our fellow citizens to the true costs of militarism, by working to change our nation's priorities, and by conducting projects to heal the wounds of war.

War Resisters League

339 Lafayette Street
New York, NY 10012
Tel: 212-228-0450
Email: wrl@warresisters.org
Website: www.warresisters.org

WRL is a pacifist organization founded in 1923. We do not support any kind of war, international or civil. We believe in nonviolence to remove all the causes of war. We produce educational resources (including The Nonviolent Activist magazine), work in coalition with other peace and justice groups, oppose conscription and all forms of militarism including ROTC, provide training in civil disobedience, war tax resistance, and other acts of putting conscience into action.

Voices in the Wilderness

1460 West Carmen Ave.
Chicago, IL 60640
Tel: 773-784-8065
Website: www.nonviolence.org/vitw

VITW is a joint US/UK campaign to end the economic sanctions against the people of Iraq. Since 1996, more than fifty delegations have traveled to Iraq to openly challenge the sanctions. Since September 2002, the Iraq Peace Team, a group of nonviolent activists, has been on the ground in Iraq standing in solidarity with the Iraqi people and working to prevent a U.S. attack.

Women's International League for Peace and Freedom

1213 Race Street, Philadelphia, PA 19107
Tel: 215-563-7110
Fax: 215-563-5527
Email: wilpf@wilpf.org
Website: www.wilpf.org

WILPF works through peaceful means to achieve world disarmament, full rights for women, racial and economic justice, and an end to all forms of violence. We seek to establish political, social, and psychological conditions that can assure peace, freedom, and justice for all.

Photograph and Drawing Credits

Page 3: Artist unknown
Page 4, upper: J.E. Taylor, J. Karst
Page 4, lower: New York Historical Society
Page 6: U.S. Army Signal Corps
Page 7, upper: Mayol
Page 7, middle: U.S. National Archives
Page 7, lower: W.A. Rogers
Page 9, upper: Karen Glynn and Eddie Becker Archive
Page 9, lower: U.S. Government (Forward March)
Page 11: Yosuke Yamahata
Page 13: U.S. Department of Defense
Page 14: Ngo Vinh Long collection
Page 15, upper and middle: U.S. Dept. of Defense
Page 20: Mary Martin

Page 24, upper and lower left: Commission of Inquiry for the International War Crimes Tribunal
Page 24, right: New York Times
Page 31: Amir Shah, Associated Press
Page 45: John Schreiber
Page 55: Harvey Richards, War Resisters League
Page 56, upper: Brian Shannon
Page 56, lower: John Gray
Page 58, upper: Bernard Edelman
Page 58, lower: Flax Hermes
Page 59: Steven Gross
Page 61: Deirdre Griswold, International Action Center

Reference Notes

1. For updated information on the U.S. military budget, see Center for Defense Information, www.cdi.org/issues/budget.

2. Giles cited in Howard Zinn, *A People's History of the United States* (New York: Harper-Collins, 1980), p. 153.

3. Zinn, pp. 125–146; Dee Brown, *Bury My Heart at Wounded Knee: An Indian History of the American West* (New York: Holt, Rinehart and Winston, 1971).

4. Black Elk cited in Brown, p. 419.

5. Zinn, pp. 147–166.

6. Denby cited in David Healy, *U.S. Expansionism: The Imperialist Urge in the 1890s* (Madison, WI: University of Wisconsin, 1970), pp. 122–123.

7. Platt cited in Healy, p. 173.

8. Roosevelt cited in Zinn, p. 290.

9. Zinn, pp. 290–305; Beveridge cited in Zinn, p. 306.

10. Beveridge cited in Healy, p. 174.

11. Beveridge cited in Rubin Westin, *Racism in U.S. Imperialism* (Columbia, SC: University of South Carolina, 1972), p. 46.

12. Zinn, pp. 305–313; Michael Parenti, *The Sword and the Dollar* (New York: St. Martins Press, 1989), pp. 42–43.

13. Zinn, pp. 290–305.

14. Hawaii: Joseph Gerson, "The Sun Never Sets," in Joseph Gerson, ed., *The Sun Never Sets— Confronting the Network of Foreign U.S. Military Bases* (Boston: South End Press, 1991), pp. 6,10; Panama: T. Harry Williams, et al., *A History of the United States [Since 1865]*, 2nd edition (New York: Alfred A. Knopf, 1965), pp. 372–373.

15. David Cooney, *A Chronology of the U.S. Navy: 1775–1965* (New York: Franklin Watts, 1965), pp. 181–257.

16. Catherine Sunshine, *The Caribbean: Struggle, Survival and Sovereignty* (Boston: South End Press, 1985), p. 32.

17. George Black, *The Good Neighbor* (New York: Pantheon Books, 1988), pp. 31–58; Sunshine, pp. 28–34.

18. Taft cited in William Appleman Williams, *Americans in a Changing World: A History of the U.S. in a Changing World* (New York: Harper and Row, 1978), pp. 123–124.

19. Report cited in Westin, p. 226.

20. Sunshine, p. 83.

21. Butler cited in Joyce Brabner, "War Is a Racket," *Real War Stories, No. 2* (Forestville, CA: Eclipse, 1991).

22. Page cited in William Foster, *Outline Political History of the Americas* (New York: International Publishers, 1951), p. 362.

23. Foster, p. 360.

24. Butler cited in Brabner.

25. CFR/State Department policy statement cited in Lawrence Shoup and William Minter, *Imperial Brain Trust: The Council on Foreign Relations and U.S. Foreign Policy* (New York: Monthly Review, 1977), p. 130.

26. CFR memorandum cited in Shoup and Minter, p. 170.

27. *Hiroshima-Nagasaki: A Pictorial Record of the Atomic Destruction* (Tokyo: Hiroshima-Nagasaki Publishing Committee, 1978), p. 17.

28. Truman cited in Paul Boyer, *By the Bombs Early Light: American Thought and Culture at the Dawn of the Atomic Age* (New York: Pantheon, 1985).

29. The bombing was also intended to preempt Soviet involvement in the war against Japan: Zinn, pp. 413–415.

30. Welch cited in Victor Perlo, *Militarism and Industry: Arms Profiteering in the Missile Age* (New York: International Publishers, 1963), p. 144.

31. Gerson, p. 12.

32. Korea International War Crimes Tribunal, "Report on U.S. Crimes in Korea: 1945–2001," (Washington, D.C.: Korea Truth Commission Task Force, 2001), p. xi; *Encyclopedia Britannica*, 1967 ed., V. 13, p. 475; *Selected Manpower Statistics, Fiscal Year 1984* (Washington D.C.: Dept. of Defense, 1985), p. 111.

33. Sunshine, p. 142; Black, p. 118.

34. Noam Chomsky, "Patterns of Intervention," in Joseph Gerson, ed., *The Deadly Connection: Nuclear War and U.S. Intervention* (Philadelphia: New Society, 1986), p. 66; Zinn, p. 469; Sean Murphy et al, *No Fire, No Thunder: The Threat of Chemical and Biological Weapons* (New York: Monthly Review, 1984), pp. 22–24, 64, 78–79; Parenti, p. 44; *Selected Manpower Statistics*; Marilyn Young, *The Vietnam Wars: 1945–1990* (New York: Harper-Collins, 1991).

35. Robert Fisk, *Pity the Nation: Lebanon at War* (Oxford University Press, 1992); Sandra Mackey, *Lebanon: Death of a Nation* (New York: Congdon & Weed, 1989).

36. Black, p. 156.

37. Schultz cited in Black, p. 156.

38. Noam Chomsky, *The Culture of Terrorism* (Boston: South End Press, 1988), p. 29; Associated Press "Libyan Court Wants Americans Arrested for 1986 Bombing," March 22, 1999.

39. Noam Chomsky, *Fateful Triangle: The United States, Israel & The Palestinians* (Cambridge, MA: South End Press, 1999).

40. William Blum, *Killing Hope: U.S. Military and CIA Interventions Since World War II* (Monroe, ME: Common Courage Press, 1995).

41. Jack Nelson-Pallmeyer, *School of Assassins* (Maryknoll, NY: Orbis Books, 1999)

42. Charles Bergquist, et al., *Violence in Colombia: The Contemporary Crisis in Historical Perspective* (Wilmington, DE: Scholarly Resources, 1992); W. M. LeoGrande and K. Sharpe, "A Plan, But No Clear Objective," *Washington Post*, April 1, 2001, p. B02; Mark Cook, "Colombia, the Politics of Escalation," *Covert Action Quarterly*, Fall/Winter 1999, No. 68.

43. Peter Wyden, *Bay of Pigs: The Untold Story* (New York: Simon and Schuster, 1979).

44. Richard Leonard, *South Africa at War: White Power and the Crisis in Southern Africa* (Westport, CT: Lawrence Hill, 1983); Richard Bloomfield, ed., *Regional Conflict and U.S. Policy: Angola and Mozambique* (Algonac, MI: Reference Publications, 1988); Alex Vines, *RENAMO: Terrorism and Mozambique* (Bloomington, IN: Indiana University Press, 1991); Joseph Hanlon and James Currey, *Mozambique: Who Calls the Shots?* (London: Zed, 1991).

45. Reagan cited in Black, p. 170.

46. John K. Cooley, "*Unholy Wars: Afghanistan, America and International Terrorism*," (London: Pluto Press, 2000).

47. David Barsamian interviews Eqbal Ahmad, *The Progressive*, Nov. 1998.

48. NSC document cited in *New York Times*, Feb. 23, 1991.

49. Doug Ireland, "Press Clips," *Village Voice*, Nov. 13, 1990.

50. Tim Wheeler, "Reagan, Noriega and Citicorp," *People's Daily World*, Feb. 25, 1988, p. 14A.

51. Kenneth Sharpe and Joseph Treaster, "Cocaine Is Again Surging Out of Panama," *New York Times*, Aug. 13, 1991, p. A1.

52. Tom Wicker, "What Price Panama?," *New York Times*, June 15, 1990; Nathaniel Sheppard, Jr., "Year Later, Panama Still Aches," *Chicago Tribune*, Dec. 16, 1990, p. 1; Associated Press, "Ex-Senator Says U.S. Massacred Panamanians" *Chicago Tribune*, Nov. 15, 1990.

53. Unnamed advisor cited in *Time*, Aug. 20, 1990.

54. State Department statement cited in Joseph Gerson, et al., "The U.S. in the Middle East," *Deadly Connection*, p. 167.

55. Michael Tanzer, *The Energy Crisis: World Struggle for Power and Wealth* (New York: Monthly Review, 1974).

56. Kissinger cited in Hans von Sponek and Denis Halliday, "The Hostage Nation," *The Guardian*, Nov. 29, 2001.

57. Carter cited in Michael Klare, *Beyond the "Vietnam Syndrome:" U.S Intervention in the 1980's* (Washington, D.C.: Institute for Policy Studies, 1980), p. 30.

58. Clyde Farnsworth, "Military Exports to Iraq Under Scrutiny, Congressional Aides Say," *New York Times*, June 24, 1991; Michael Klare, "Behind Desert Storm: The New Military Paradigm," *Technology Review*, May–June 1991, p. 36; Philip Shenon, "Declaration Lists Companies That Sold Chemicals to Iraq," *New York Times*, Dec. 21, 2002; Christopher Dickey and Evan Thomas, "How Saddam Happened," *Newsweek*, Sept. 23, 2002.

59. Philip Green "Who Really Shot Down Flight 655," *The Nation*, Aug. 13–20, 1988, pp. 125–126.

60. Glaspie cited in Christopher Hitchins, "Real Politics in the Gulf: A Game Gone Tilt," in Micah Sifry and C. Cerf, eds., *Gulf War Reader: History, Documents, Opinions* (New York: Times Books / Random House, 1991), pp. 116–117.

61. Hitchins; Bush cited in *Newsweek*, Jan. 7, 1991, p.19.

62. Michael Klare, "High Death Weapons of the Gulf War," *The Nation*, June 3, 1991; Malcolm Browne, "Allies Are Said to Choose Napalm for Strikes on Iraqi Fortifications," *New York Times*, Feb. 23, 1991; John Donnelly, "Iraqi cancers offer clues to Gulf War Syndrome: Uranium residue a prime suspect," *Miami Herald*, April 6, 1998

63. Mark Fireman, "Eyewitnesses Report Misery, Devastation in the Cities of Iraq," *Seattle Times*, Feb. 5, 1991; George Esper, "500 Die in Bombed Shelter in Baghdad," *Chicago Sun Times*, Feb. 13, 1991; David Evans, "Study: Hyperwar Devastated Iraq," *Chicago Tribune*, May 29, 1991.

64. "War Summary: Closing the Gate," *New York Times*, Feb. 28, 1991, p. A6; Associated Press, "Army Tanks Buried Iraqi Soldiers Alive," *Greeley Tribune*, Sept. 12, 1991.

65. Bush cited in Robert Borosage, "How Bush kept the guns from turning into butter," *Rolling Stone*, Feb. 21, 1991, p. 20.

66. Ramsey Clark, *The Fire This Time: U.S. War Crimes in the Gulf* (New York: International Action Center, 2002) pp. 64–64, 209; Thomas J. Nagy, "The Secret Behind the Sanctions: How the U.S. Intentionally Destroyed Iraq's Water Supply," *The Progressive*, Sept. 2001.

67. John Pilger, "Collateral Damage," in Anthony Arnove, ed., *Iraq Under Siege: The Deadly Impact of Sanctions and War* (Cambridge, MA: South End Press, 2000) pp. 59–66.

68. Thomas Hayes, "Oil's Inconvenient Bonanza," *New York Times*, Jan. 27, 1991, p. F4.

69. Tanzer.

70. National Coalition to Stop U.S. Intervention in the Middle East, *Stop the War*, 1991.

71. R. Barnet and J. Cavanagh, "Unequally Sharing the Costs and Dividends of War," *The Real Costs of War* (Washington, D.C.: Institute for Policy Studies, May 1991), p. 3.

72. Colman McCarthy, "U.S. First in Exports to Killing Fields," *Washington Post*, Sept. 10, 1991, p. C12; Clyde Farnsworth, "White House Seeks to Renew Credits for Arms Exports," *New York Times*, March 18, 1991, p. A1.

73. Baker cited in William Hartung, "Relighting the Mideast Fuse," *New York Times*, Sept. 20, 1991.

74. Hartung.

75. Noam Chomsky, *A New Generation Draws the Line: Kosovo, East Timor and the Standards of the West* (London: Verso), p. 11.

76. Nick Wood, "U.S. 'Covered Up' for Kosovo Ally," *The London Observer,* September 10, 2000; Norman Kempster, "Crisis in Yugoslavia, Rebel Force May Prove to be a Difficult Ally," *Los Angeles Times*, April 1, 1999. Ultimatum: Diana Johnstone, "Hawks and Eagles: 'Greater NATO' Flies to the Aid of 'Greater Albania,'" *Covert Action Quarterly*, Spring/Summer, 1999, No. 67, p. 6–12.

77. Noam Chomsky, *The New Military Humanism: Lessons from Kosovo* (Monroe, ME: Common Courage Press, 1999).

78. Bin Laden cited in *Wall Street Journal*, 2001-10-7.

79. Bush cited in "The President's Words," *The Los Angeles Times*, Sept. 22, 2001.

80. One investigator has estimated that U.S. bombs killed between 3100 and 3600 Afghan civilians and thousands more died because bombing cut off relief supplies. Marc Herold, "U.S. bombing and Afghan civilian deaths: The official neglect of unworthy bodies," *International Journal of Urban and Regional Research*, Sept. 2002, pp. 626–634. Also see: http://pubpages.unh.edu/~mwherold.

81. Bosch cited in Alexander Cockburn, "The Tribulations of Joe Doherty," *Wall Street Journal*, reprinted in the *Congressional Record*, August 3, 1990, p. E2639.

82. Cockburn; John Rice, "Man with CIA Links Accused of Plotting to Kill Castro," Associated Press, Nov. 18, 2000; Frances Robles and Glenn Garvin, "Four Held in Plot Against Castro," *Miami Herald*, Nov. 19, 2000; Jill Mullin, "The Burden of a Violent History," *Miami New Times*, April 20, 2000.

83. Joe Conason, "The Bush Pardons," http://archive. salon.com/news/col/cona/ 2001/02/27/pardons/

84. Bosch cited in Cockburn.

85. William Blum, *Killing Hope: U.S. Military and CIA Interventions Since World War II* (Monroe, ME: Common Courage Press, 1995).

86. For updated information on post-9-11 restrictions on civil liberties see the American Civil Liberties Union's website: www.aclu.org/safeandfree

87. Joshua Cohen, "An Interview with Ted Postol: What's Wrong with Missile Defense," *Boston Review*, Oct./Nov. 2001; David Sanger, "Washington's New Freedom and New Worries in the Post-ABM-Treaty Era," *New York Times*, Dec. 15, 2001.

88. For updated information on U.S. nuclear weapons policies see the Physicians for Social Responsibility website: http://www.psr.org/.

89. R. Jeffrey Smith, "U.S. Urged to Cut 50% of A-Arms: Soviet Breakup Is Said to Allow Radical Shift in Strategic Targeting," *Washington Post*, Jan. 6, 1991, p. A1. Also see: Michael Gordon, "U.S. Nuclear Plan Sees New Weapons and New Targets," *New York Times*, March 10, 2002.

90. Judith Miller, "U.S. Seeks Changes in Germ War Pact," *New York Times*, Nov. 1, 2001; William Broad and Judith Miller, "U.S. Recently Produced Anthrax in a Highly Lethal Powder Form," *New York Times*, Dec. 13, 2001.

91. William Broad and Judith Miller, "*Germs: Biological Weapons and America's Secret War*," (New York: Simon & Schuster, 2001); William Blum.

92. For updated information on U.S. and world military spending, see the Center for Defense Information website: http://www.cdi.org.

93. Center for Defense Information, *2001–2002 Military Almanac*, p. 35; http://www.cdi.org.

94. Center for Defense Information, http://www.cdi.org/issues/milspend.html

95. Michael Renner, *National Security: The Economic and Environmental Dimensions* (Washington, D.C.: World Watch Institute, 1989), p. 23.

96. The War Resisters League's annual analysis of total U.S. military expenditures can be found at: http://www.warresisters.org/piechart.htm.

97. The War Resisters League estimates that about 46% of federal tax revenues are used for military expenses (ibid.). Total 2000 Federal individual income tax revenues ($1,004,500,000,000) multiplied by 46%, divided by 104,705,000 households = $4,413 (http://www.census.gov/prod/ 2002pubs/ 01statab/fedgov.pdf, pp. 21 and 305).

98. Timothy Saasta, et al., *America's Third Deficit: Too Little Investment in People and Infrastructure* (Washington, D.C.: Center for Community Change, 1991).

99. *Fact Sheet No. 3* (Boston: Jobs With Peace Campaign, 1990).

100. Saasta; Institute for Policy Studies, *Harvest of Shame: Ten Years of Conservative Misrule* (Washington, D.C.: Institute for Policy Studies,